THE
PLEASURES OF CIGAR
SMOKING

This delightful old whaling chanty is still sung today by folk singers, but its origin is lost in the past. Reportedly, it goes back to about 1600.

'Twas off the blue Canary Isles, one glorious summer's day
I sat upon the quarter deck, and whiffed my cares away.
And as the volumed smoke arose, like incense in the air,
I breathed a sigh to think, in sooth, it was my last cigar.
It was my last cigar,
It was my last cigar,
I breathed a sigh to think, in sooth,
It was my last cigar.
I've seen the land of all I love, fade in the distance dim,
I've watched above the blighted heart, where once fond hope
        had been.
But I've never known a sorrow that could with that compare
As off the blue Canary Isles, I smoked my last cigar.

THE PLEASURES OF CIGAR SMOKING

BY J. B. BACK

R

A Rutledge Book

Photo Credits:
UPI—pp. 14, 53, 85.
Cigar Institute—p. 29.
New York Public Library Picture Collection—pp. 50-51, 60.
Walter Storck Studios, Inc—cover.

Prepared and produced by Rutledge Books, Inc.
Library of Congress Catalog Card Number 76-146741
Printed in the United States of America

About the Author

If anyone knows anything about quality cigars in this country, it is Mr. J. B. Back. Good cigars were part of his life, and still are.

Mr. Back learned the trade as a teen-ager, back in 1904. He was then working for his uncle in Brooklyn, New York—wrapping, selecting and packing the product. When he had mastered the finer points of cigar making—six years later—he opened up his own shop. It was then a modest little establishment, with three employees.

Once launched in the cigar business, Mr. Back could no longer be stopped. Realizing the endless and fascinating possibilities, he became a dedicated cigar man. When he was 28, he opened up a larger shop, this time in Fulton Street, Brooklyn, and the number of his employees had risen to 25.

But he was not satisfied with that. In September 1919 he bought a whole building in Kingston, New York. Mr. Back believed in the future of cigars, and his confidence was justified. He bought a larger factory at Wilbur Avenue, also in Kingston.

Mr. Back must have been on pretty goods terms with Governor Al Smith of New York State, because in 1930 the governor signed the first lease for him in New York City's Empire State Building. So, for quite a number of years, Mr. Back sold his fine cigars from a store in the largest building in the world.

To this day, Mr. Back's name stands for craftsmanship, judgment, quality and flavor in the making of cigars. He is still active and interested in many things. However, when it comes to smoking, he always returns to his first love—a fine cigar.

Contents

1

Call them by their rightful name

By way of introduction

Some call them stogies.

Some call them ropes, segars, cheroots, cabbages, black beauties or broom handles.

Some call them by their rightful name: cigars.

Whatever men call them, an oft-heard saying applies to cigars today, namely, "They don't make them the way they used to." This is true. It is also no cause for lament. There is nothing lost. In the United States in particular, custom cigar makers are turning out finer products than they ever have before.

There is something new going on in domestic quality cigars, something exciting, something which will enable American cigar producers to maintain forever the quality lead they now hold.

Surprisingly perhaps, this new level of domestic cigar quality has come about as result of political upheaval.

As everyone must know by now, the Fidel Castro take-over of Cuba eventually led to the United States embargo on all imports from this island, cigars and unprocessed tobacco included. The embargo created a vacuum in the American cigar tobacco supply. American firms were compelled to search elsewhere to supplement the prime domestic American supplies they have traditionally used.

This hunt occurred simultaneously with the fortunate defection from Castro communism of experienced Cuban tobacco people from the island. Entire families of growers fled by legal and illegal means to nearby Latin American countries. The makers fled also. Many came to the United States. They were absorbed by the industry here. The industry was delighted to have them.

Both growers and makers brought with them all of the expertise developed over three centuries of cigar making on their island. The growers brought one additional thing.

They brought tobacco seeds.

They planted these seeds in their new countries bordering the Caribbean Sea. How did the resulting crops compare with those they once produced in their homeland? Surprise—the new crops were superior. New climates and soils improved quality and yield.

At this same time, growers already established in other Latin American countries decided that the tobacco vacuum in the United States represented something for them also: a chance to help fill the vacuum and thereby earn bundles of money.

Now, prior to the embargo, some of these countries (Honduras and Mexico, to name two) enjoyed no reputation for producing great tobacco. If they had any reputation at all, it was for mediocre leaf and cigars.

Certain other countries did already enjoy reputations for quality tobacco prior to the embargo. However, for one reason or another, they had never developed a substantial market in the United States. The vacuum also inspired their growers to examine this country more closely.

A happy trio

Three developments were taking place simultaneously then. One, Cuban growers were beginning to produce quality leaf in other countries. Two, countries growing poor tobacco

11

began reassessing and upgrading their efforts to grow good tobacco. Three, countries already growing good tobacco were trying to grow better tobacco.

The result? Within a few years there were new high-quality leaves coming into the United States from formerly untapped sources. The new leaves demonstrated smoking qualities never before seen.

Custom cigar makers today are importing much of their filler, binder and wrapper leaf from these new sources. New tobaccos are appearing today along with the great traditional domestic American growths in fine-quality cigars. The custom-grade product has never been of higher quality.

One manufacturer says he wishes the changes had come about years earlier.

A beginning smoker purchasing cigars today hears tobacconists name countries he may have never associated with cigars: Mexico, Brazil, Santo Domingo, Honduras, Nicaragua and Cameroon in Africa. This last-named country exports the best wrapper available anywhere today. Cameroon wrapper is also the most expensive. Any cigar wrapped in Cameroon leaf is almost certain to be a beautiful cigar by all smoking standards.

The experienced smoker will not find the names strange. He is used to hearing them by now. For several years he has been enjoying good blends of imported and domestic tobacco in his cigars.

There were other spin-off benefits from the exodus. "Some of us began experimenting with new blends, using filler from one country, binder from another, wrapper from still another, in ways we'd never tried before," one cigar company executive says. "And what happened was, some brands which had been only so-so up to that time turned out to be terrific when some of the new tobaccos were added."

The new tobaccos also spawned an entire generation of new cigars never blended before. One ex-Cuban maker with 50 years' experience at his trade developed a new one recently and terms it a "cigar everyone likes."

The formula: Brazilian, Honduran and Nicaraguan mixed short filler; Connecticut binder; a good Cameroon wrapper.

12

One of his associates feels his description is too modest. He feels that it should be called "super cigar" instead.

This book makes an unashamed pitch for quality cigars as one of the good things of life along with fine wines and classic cars. "Quality cigars" is, frankly, an unashamedly snobbish term. As it is used here it includes domestic custom-blended products as well as some imports. The term excludes low-quality, mass-produced cigars which, no matter what their manufacturers claim, are still low-quality mass-produced cigars.

And, not to put too long an ash on this discussion of new tobaccos and new cigars, Cuba must finally be dismissed as a once-great empire now fallen. It is considered unlikely that she will ever challenge American custom cigars for supremacy again.

Indeed, on the quality level we speak of here, some experts say she was not a serious challenge to begin with.

Like wines, like cigars

Cigars can be likened to fine wines. Indeed, when tobacco was first brought to Europe in the 15th and 16th centuries, a smoker was said to be taking "a drink of smoke." 13

Just as wine grapes of one region are superior to those of another area, some cigar tobaccos outrank others. And just as some vintage years are better than others, cigar years vary also. The cigars of the 1950s, for instance, were said to be especially good.

As different wines give off individual bouquets, different cigars generate individual aromas. The connoisseur can tell at one sniff whether a tobacco is of Jamaican or Floridian origin.

As some wines are best drunk at certain times of the day rather than at others, so, too, is there a time for each type of cigar. Many men consider the portly corona with a dark maduro wrapper the only cigar to smoke after a leisurely dinner.

And as lengthy trial and error (and many sour bottles) precedes sound wine judgment, lengthy trial and error (and many volcanic cigars) nurtures sound cigar sense.

Book learning is no shortcut, but it helps. This book is filled, bound and wrapped with fact and opinion valuable to both the old smoker and the new.

A taste for and knowledge of vintage wine can be said to indicate a type of man and the caliber of his sophistication. So can taste for and knowledge of cigars. Can such a man be described? Yes, and quite accurately.

He is youthful in spirit as well as in years. He is active and interested in his world regardless of age. (Note: He is *not* cast in the classic image of the cigar chewer whose cigar is dead ash at one end and wet, bitten flat as a fishtail, at the other. True, there are such men who smoke cigars, and hopefully even they can learn from such a book as this.)

The quality cigar smoker may drive an MG, crew on deep-water racing sloops, sky dive from airplanes, drive a Triumph motorcycle, breed Irish setters, golf like Jack Nicklaus, play the guitar like Bob Dylan.

On the other hand, to be quite honest about it, the quality cigar smoker may be no more exciting, or excitable, than the next-door neighbor. Cigars, good cigars, are not limited to the aristocracy or the sophisticated, though the smoking of them can certainly enhance a man's image. In any case, the cigar

14

Four famous cigar smokers: Paul Newman (with inanimate friend), Hermione Gingold (who played a story writer on "Ironside"), Tom Jones (at a London press party) and Red Skelton (who "plays" his cigar like a piccolo).

smoker—steeplejack, yachtsman, banker, clerk or baseball player —is basically a man with a sense of fine taste.

Hopefully, both connoisseur and beginner (and those smokers who fall somewhere in between those two categories) will find meaningful and helpful material here which will enhance their enjoyment of cigars.

Fact and fiction

For instance, at one time or another almost every smoker has pondered the origin of the word "cigar." Our chapter on history reveals that German scholars believed the strange word to be of Mayan origin. And since history sometimes includes legend, there is an account of the Havana "cigar girls" and how they once supposedly used their bare thighs as a tool in cigar making.

And has anyone ever smoked a cigar without wondering how the devil the thing was made anyway? The chapters describing cultivation, curing and manufacture constitute a cigar-making primer.

15

These chapters go into detail about cigar fillers and explain why a cigar filled with tobacco products the industry calls "scrap" is no cigar at all by custom standards. ("Filler" is the center tobacco in a cigar, somewhat comparable to the tobacco part of a cigarette. A wrap-around "binder" layer, followed by an outer "wrapper" layer, holds the filler together, as the paper of a cigarette contains the tobacco. Filler, binder, wrapper: these are the three basic parts of a cigar.)

Unfortunately, there is no simple, universal rule for choosing the perfect specimen. There are, however, common-sense criteria for choice and selection which the beginning smoker can follow, and from which the experienced cigar person departs only according to taste and mood. The chapters on buying, storing and smoking technique provide such pointers.

For instance, why should a man trust a tobacconist who keeps a thermometer and a moisture indicator in his cigar storage compartment? And why should a man run from the tobacconist who advises storing cigars in the refrigerator?

The health aspects

Recent findings about the health hazards of cigarette smoking are a matter of concern to anyone who uses tobacco, and these are covered here, too. Public Health Service Publication No. 1103 (better known as *Smoking and Health*), published in 1964 by United States Surgeon General Luther Terry, states the cause for concern for cigarette smokers only too clearly. However, as the final chapter points out in review of the Surgeon General's report and other recent findings, the man who smokes cigars has only minimal cause for alarm. The number of cases of cancer (of the larynx, in particular) associated with cigar and pipe smoking was regarded as "not yet large enough for judgment."

Perhaps the main reason for the good marks earned by cigars is that cigar smokers do not inhale. They derive their pleasures through smell and taste rather than the charge that nicotine inhaling puts into the bloodstream. The Surgeon General's report suggests, in fact, that lung cancer and cigars can only be linked when the cigar smoker inhales.

Also included in this book is a glossary of tobacco terms that are useful and important in selecting the best cigars.

One entry is the word "stogie."

Ironically, the stogie was one of America's first custom-made cigars. It was often of superior quality, before the word became a label given today to the foul kind of smoke often referred to as *El Ropo*.

The men moving west in the great wagon trains of the mid-19th century brought along "makings"—that is, loose tobacco with which to roll their own cigars as needed. Their wagons were the seemingly indestructible "Prairie Schooners," the Conestogas, named after their place of manufacture, Conestoga, Pennsylvania. The wagoneers who rolled their own could think of no better name of quality to give their cigars than that of their wagons. So they called their good cigars Conestogas, and the name was eventually shortened to "stogies."

"Stogie" is but one of scores of names given to cigars over the years. And the emergence of such names represents but one part of the long history of cigars.

16

2

A matter of choice

One man's panatela
is another man's stogie

During the Franco-Prussian War (the story goes) a young
dragoon lay dying. He called out to no one in particular for
something, anything, to take his mind from his final agony.

The "Iron Chancellor" of Prussia himself, Otto von Bismarck, was riding past at that moment. He dismounted, took
a massive Dutch cigar from his case, lit it and placed it between the wounded man's teeth. Bismarck sighed as he did so.
The cigar was his last. He had been saving it to smoke when
the day's battle was done.

The dragoon smiled, puffed the cigar fiercely and, just
before closing his eyes forever, muttered, "Please tell Herr von
Bismarck I thank him profoundly, but next time I'd prefer
something from the Caribbean."

The incident illustrates again a principle that could be
called "The First Law of Cigars." It is this:

One man cannot choose a cigar for another and hope to
please him completely.

The parallel for judging fine wine comes to mind. One
man may insist that only a Burgundy possesses enough body to
support a dinner of rare roast beef. Another may feel the Bur-

gundy to be barbaric, far too heavy for rare roast. He may choose one of the lighter Beaujolais reds.

Neither wine (if both are of good vintage and carefully produced and bottled) can be said to be the better. The choice is a matter of personal taste. Actually, with rare beef, either can be an exciting partner.

So it is with choosing and enjoying cigars. One man's favorite can be another man's tear-gas bomb.

As no two gourmets share the same preferences in wines, no two men share exactly the same tastes in cigars.

Examples:

Aristotle Onassis, who sometimes gives the appearance of owning half the world's ships, is a double-corona man. The double corona is sometimes called a "chair rung" or "broomstick." Eight to nine inches long, it is truly a classic tycoon's cigar.

Rainier, Prince of Monaco, prefers Lonsdales. The Lonsdale is also a large cigar but of more modest dimensions than the double corona, and more graceful in appearance.

18

A pointless debate

A double corona-Lonsdale debate is pointless. Each cigar possesses smoking characteristics the other does not. Each fulfills esthetic demands the other cannot. Both can be great cigars, equal in their capacity for bringing pleasure if the two are of equal quality.

But what of the man who is not a connoisseur and simply wishes to choose some decent cigars for himself?

Are there rules he can apply to judging aroma? Are there yardsticks of quality in manufacture? Are there brand names which mean something?

Bet a custom corona on this: yes.

There are definite criteria to follow in selecting cigars. They are sound. They are fundamental. They have been honed and polished by trial and error over centuries. They are especially valuable to the beginner or to the smoker who has already begun and is now broadening his familiarity with cigars. To this person (him or her), some advice:

Study these guidelines. Individual good taste is mentioned frequently as being the final arbiter in cigar choice. Good taste will follow learning almost without effort.

The late General Douglas MacArthur was one of the choosiest cigar smokers of all time, so choosy in fact that he changed his ways rather than compromise his standards.

During World War II, production and shipping restrictions pinched the supply of quality custom-mades. After suffering through many bad ones, the general made a drastic decision for a cigar lover. Rather than smoke any more bad ones, he gave them up altogether and turned instead to the corncob pipe. This was a random choice, another historical accident, but had he employed a division of public relations men to tailor a heroic image, he could not have chosen a better personal symbol.

When the first photographs were published in 1942 showing the general firmly clenching a corncob pipe and wearing a sweaty cap with mildewed visor and braid, the troops loved it and the people back home choked with emotion. The corncob pipe was all Middle America in image; solid, dependable, enduring. The man smoking it appeared to be all hero.

Today MacArthur would never have had to make such a switch. The selection of custom cigars is as wide as anyone would wish. The combination of sizes, shapes and leaf varieties in available products is vast enough as it is. Men who know cigars say many of these custom products (both domestic and foreign imports) are equal or superior to some of the Caribbean cigar tobaccos. They always have been, but few people took the pains to learn this.

The art of knowing

The art of knowing cigars, however, is simply a matter of serious questioning and research in tobacco shops. Granted, it involves trial and error; many a *"corona terribila"* will be smoked before the process is mastered.

To begin at the beginning:

To choose a cigar, a smoker must first know the three basic terms by which cigars are categorized:

Brand name
Type, or shape
Color of leaf

To explain the three terms and their use:

The brand name is just that, a maker's identification, such as Campbell's in soups and Ford in cars. For demonstration's sake, one fine cigar name is named Brevas.

The type or shape designation describes in a word the profile of the cigar. The panatela, for instance, is perhaps the most popular type of full-sized cigar today because of its lean, guided-missile look.

The third term is leaf color. When specified, this reveals the tobacco strength a smoker likes. Cigar-tobacco strength is usually associated with its color. There is one general rule of thumb:

When we speak of strength we mean, essentially, durability. Leaf cured to maduro colorado color, for example, is a rich brown and in the medium-strength range. The name literally means "reddish ripe" in Spanish. A Brevas panatela maduro colorado, therefore, is a slim, rich-brown, medium-strong cigar.

There is no need to elaborate further on brand names, but type and leaf color are subjects requiring more substantial coverage.

Some experts view every variation in shape as a new type to be added to the chart. Forget this. Such a chart would become totally unmanageable. The Caribbean area alone once produced 960 shapes and sizes in varying leaf colors. You can imagine the potential proliferation of terms this would entail.

Then, too, there is always a kind of cigar, such as the torpedo, which virtually defies classification. The football-shaped torpedo, seldom manufactured today, is pointed at the ends but fat around the middle. Does it classify as a perfecto shape (i.e., tapered at both ends)? No, it is not a perfecto. It is a torpedo, and a torpedo is what it has always been.

Three basic shapes

A classification breakdown is necessary nonetheless. For

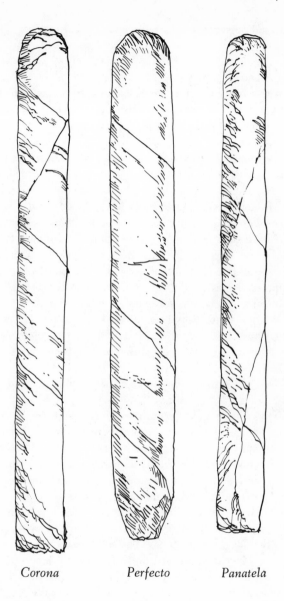

Corona   *Perfecto*   *Panatela*

all practical purposes there are three basic cigar types or shapes:

Corona

Perfecto

Panatela

Except for "character" cigars such as the torpedo, all other types have evolved from these three. No matter what their length, thickness or profile, all are variations on these three basic styles.

There are a few experts, of course, who claim this reduction to three is an oversimplification. To the three mentioned above they would add the Lonsdale, the culebra and the demitasse. Most, however, object to such a detailed breakdown.

The Lonsdale, for one, does not make it as a separate and basic type. Its shape is too much like that of a corona.

Like the torpedo, the culebra is another character cigar, being flat and braided together in threes. It stands alone, hardly a true prototype, as are the perfecto, panatela and corona.

And the demitasse is really only a midget corona.

Welcome to diversity of opinion. The industry has thrived on diversity of brand, type and leaf. Why not on opinion also? When there are no longer any differences in the cigar industry, there can only be indifference, cigar makers feel.

The three basic types and their identifying characteristics are as follows:

Corona: The head (mouth end) is rounded and closed. "Closed" means that the smoker must cut or break a hole open before lighting in order to draw smoke through. The corona body is cylindrical; the sides are parallel and straight. The tuck (lighting end) is cut (trimmed) and shows filler-leaf end grain. The standard corona measures between five and a half and six inches in length. It is the most popular type today.

Perfecto: The head is tapered to a rounded point and is closed. The body is cylindrical. The tuck is tapered and can be either cut or closed. The standard perfecto length is five inches. Tobacconists and custom makers say that the perfecto popularity is fading these days and it may eventually disappear.

Panatela: The silhouette is characterized by a distinctly lean look. The classic panatela body is a true cylinder without any tapering at either head or foot. The panatela sometimes does have a "shoulder" (a slight "stepping in" to a lesser diameter at the head end). The head is sometimes rounded, sometimes cut. The tuck is cut. Both head and tuck can show filler-leaf end grain. Five inches, give or take a quarter, is standard panatela length. The panatela is fast approaching the perfecto in popularity (a popularity which is fading anyway) and may soon overtake the corona.

It should be noted that cigars tend to lose their cylindrical shapes and become squarish as a result of being packed tightly pressed together in bunches and boxes.

A shade different

Now, in moving to leaf coloration, one ought to keep certain important things in mind:

Color uniformity inside and out is a sign of cigar quality. It is carried beyond single cigars to entire boxfuls. Each box is packed with cigars as nearly the same in shade as possible so that strength will be uniform throughout. Cigars on the top row of each quality box are even more fastidiously chosen for uniform shade, for the sake of appearance. The cigars on the lower levels may vary slightly in color.

Color is no indication of nicotine content, although it has been held that dark leaf contains more nicotine than the light does. In reality, however, sometimes the lighter the leaf, the higher the nicotine content.

Color *is* the promise of graceful aging to come. Light-colored cigars do not as a rule mature and keep as long as dark cigars do. The lighter ones tend to dry earlier. For a light candela the maximum aging time is from eight months to a year, according to many tobacconists. After that time, they feel, the quality fades.

The industry generally accepts seven traditional color classifications as the most workable number. Taste and preference still come first, before selecting color. One custom manufacturer's claro may be browner than the claro of another, but both will be claro. The color classifications are closely observed throughout the industry.

The smoker choosing a cigar by color will find the follow-

23

ing list accurate and easy to use. Here are the seven traditional colors, from lightest to darkest:

Double claro: A light green in color. The mildest of cigar tobaccos, growing in popularity in the United States. Also called claro-claro or clarissimo or claro superlativo or candela. Claro is the Spanish adjective for "light," pertaining to color.

Claro: Greenish-brown or near-khaki in color. Still the most popular mild cigar tobacco in the United States. Noted for its delicate aroma and easy smoking characteristics. It lights readily and sustains its flame.

Colorado claro: Light-brown leaf, noticeably darker than claro. A little richer-tasting than the earlier two claros. In Spanish, "colorado claro" means, roughly, "reddish light."

Colorado: Reddish-brown-to-brown leaf. A little richer in taste, considerably stronger in aroma than the preceding colors.

Maduro colorado: Reddish brown to brownish black. Medium strength. "Maduro" is the Spanish adjective meaning "ripe." To say it again, "maduro colorado" roughly means "reddish ripe."

24

Maduro: Definite brown-black. Hearty, full taste and aroma; generally not enjoyable to beginning smokers. Maduro and maduro colorado are not too popular in the United States and Britain.

Oscuro: Black or close to it. Very full taste. Is said to be the teeth of the tobacco plant—that is, all bite. Only slight aroma. It was popular until the beginning of the 19th century. It is seldom seen today in American products. Oscuro is the Spanish adjective for "dark," "gloomy" or "dim." Oscuro leaf is sometimes called *negro,* meaning "black."

Some of the above tobaccos are also identified by commercial names for their colors. Maduro colorado is popular as wrapper in England and has become known through long use as "English Market Selection."

Popular in the United States

Candela is popular as wrapper in United States products, and cigars so wrapped are often called "candelas." Candela could technically be called a fine claro. It is a light, pale green.

The color of cigar tobacco is determined mainly by two factors: 1. position of the leaf on the growing plant; 2. curing methods applied to it. The various shades can be as lovely to the eye as they are indicative of strength: the French impressionist painter Pierre Renoir sought to match his browns with those of the colorados—he held them to be so rich.

Knowing the language of brand name, type and color, one can move ahead to consider the finer points involved in choosing cigars to taste. Here are the basics, agreed upon wherever men smoke cigars:

■ Choosing a tobacconist. How can one determine whether the man is competent? By the length of time he has been in business, for one thing. Men who like quality cigars can be harsh judges and a shop will not last if its products are inferior.

One sign of a good shop: the tobacconist will replace without objection any cigars found to be faulty.

One sign of a dubious shop: a salesman who recommends such measures as storing cigars in deep freezers. Some do advise this. Pay no attention to this. Abrupt changes in temperature and humidity can open brutal cracks in the leaf.

25

■ Temperature and humidity. Cigars that are not stored at a cool temperature and moderate humidity are a poor choice. What is cool? What is moderate? Again, the experts do not agree upon precise figures, but they are fairly close in their estimates.

A noted European seller, who numbers members of the aristocracy, financiers and other "Very Important Persons" among his customers, claims that 68 to 77 degrees F. and 60 to 67 percent humidity are ideal. (Off the subject but interesting is the fact that one of his VIP clients once "skipped out" owing him a sizable bill. He was a Russian named V. I. Lenin.)

A celebrated British firm with branches in the big cities the world over allows no leeway in its temperature and humidity control. The temperature in the cigar lockers is always kept at precisely 66 degrees F. The humidity is held at precisely 60 percent.

If they have not been kept at a reasonable temperature and humidity, cigars are apt to be either too dry or too moist for comfortable smoking.

A dry cigar burns fast and hot and the smoke may irritate tender mouth and throat membranes. Also, the wrapper of a dry cigar is apt to unravel in the process of smoking.

A cigar which is too moist may prove difficult to light.

■ Cigars bearing identifiable national characteristics. With practice over the years, a smoker can learn to sort them out blindfolded, naming the country of origin of any cigar on first puff. A few examples:

The Canary Islands cigar is now frequently offered in the United States as a substitute for the Antillean product. It is regarded as tasting almost the same and being just as fine.

United States custom cigars are growing in reputation as being of similar taste and quality to some highly touted foreign imports, and many are even thought to be superior.

Jamaican cigars are generally more expensive than the above but not as smooth.

The twisty Italian cheroots are unmistakable. They are salami-hard. Their wrappers are secured by rice-flour paste in the rolling. They are difficult to keep ignited and volcanic to smoke.

English smokers like their pipe tobacco damp and their cigars dry; smokers of most other countries prefer the reverse. There is an apocryphal explanation for the English preference. When cigars were first introduced into England there was little demand for them. Stocks became brittle and dry on the store shelves. Not men to lose money on their inventory investments, English tobacconists persuaded their customers that cigars were best smoked dry and brittle, being only then fully seasoned. Myth became preference, and the taste for dry cigars prevails in England to this day.

The cigars of India were once said to be "doped" with opium, because tobacco and opium crops were rotated in alternate years on the same fields. The rotation might have improved plant size and yield, but it is questionable that the characteristics of one plant ever significantly affected the other.

■ Ash is important. Quality cigars produce gray ash, inferior cigars whiter ash. A long ash buildup indicates care in the manufacture of the cigar. A flicked ash should leave a sharp, glowing point. The sharper the point, the better the cigar.

26

The twisted, salami-hard cheroot isn't the choosy smoker's delight.

■ Quality of tobacco. The Internal Revenue Service defines a cigar for taxation purposes as being "any roll of tobacco wrapped in tobacco." This sounds simple and clear enough, in theory. In practice many cigars satisfy the definition only on technicality. Their fillers are inferior. Their binders and wrappers are sometimes man-made.

There are three kinds of filler:

1. Long filler, composed of strips of tobacco leaf often as long as the cigar itself.

2. Short filler, composed of shorter lengths, which lend themselves more readily to machine production.

3. Scrap filler, composed of tobacco leaf ground to bits.

The long-filler cigar is acknowledged best in just about every way. In the United States the long-filler cigars today are almost all custom grades.

27

Three fine formulas

There are three basic cigar composition formulas, listed here in order of quality. Again, first quality is found almost exclusively in the custom grades.

1. Cigars of long filler, natural tobacco leaf binder and natural tobacco leaf wrapper.

2. Cigars of short filler, natural leaf binder and natural leaf wrapper.

3. Either of the above two, with homogenized tobacco leaf (known as "sheet") substituted for natural leaf in binders and sometimes wrappers. The short-filled, sheet-bound cigars are the least expensive. They are also the least satisfying.

Certain cigars are made of scrap filler and sheet wrapper,

without a binder layer. These prove fragile and tend to crumble under firm touch. They can be held together satisfactorily only by being fitted with plastic mouth tips.

If you really want to know the insides of a cigar, the thing to do is to dissect it. Split it lengthwise with a razor, spreading the contents along the split. Filler type will be evident immediately. So will wrapper and binder as you separate the parts.

Custom grades may hold together even when they are split. Their natural binders and wrappers grip the longer fillers generally used. The cheaper scrap-filled and sheet-bound specimens crumble.

■ The cigar band. It is not a sign of quality. Poor cigars are sold both with and without bands. Fine cigars are sold both with and without bands. When a cigar appears with a band, it is usually because the maker preferred to market it that way, and that is all.

■ Cigar sizes and shapes. Choose cigar shapes that complement the face. For example, plump smokers should avoid the fat corona, choosing a panatela instead. The thinner cigar will lend slimness to the face.

■ A different cigar for different times of day. Again, choice is a matter of smoker preference and taste, but there are some guidelines.

In the morning: something mild and short is best. Such a cigar is not likely to shake up the taste buds before lunch. A good Honduran cigar is recommended. American-made "short" or "small" cigars (now so popular) are not, unless they come from some custom establishment. There is a reason for the bad marks: scrap insides, sheet wrappers. Also, they are often mentholated or perfumed to give off a sweet aroma and taste, covering the harshness of inferior tobacco products. These are known as "candy cigars."

In the afternoon: this is the time for something heartier, in the claro or colorado color and strength range, and of substantial size for a substantial smoke.

In the evening, following dinner: almost anything that suits the taste is proper. Something full-bodied and long-burning is most satisfactory. If a smoker is having several cigars, the wine-bibbing strategy applies here: start with light, move pro-

28

Cigars chosen with care deserve a good humidor.

gressively to the richer. A corona colorado is a good average choice if there is to be but one cigar after dinner.

A 45-minute smoke

A quality cigar burns from 45 minutes to an hour from igniting it to snuffing it out depending upon length. While burning it is said to "cruise" or "live."

A fresh, quality cigar will not show stains or mildew. There may be small discolored spots in the wrapper leaf, but disregard them. Some flecking occurs naturally in growth. The difference between stains and natural spots is easy to detect. The stains resemble water splotches on wallpaper, the spots are small and clean.

A ragged or unraveled wrapper indicates that the cigar is dry. If it is mushy to the touch, it is wet and will be difficult to light.

Most cigars wrapped in leaf showing ribs and veins come from the lower part of the plant and are second-class products.

Freshness of course can be tested by touch. A superior cigar will have a springy feel when pinched between thumb and forefinger. No dimples will remain after the pinch, the cigar shaft assuming its original shape.

If a cigar carries a cellophane moisture jacket, remove it. Then hold the cigar to your ear, rolling it gently between thumb and fingers while you listen. The fresh cigar will rustle when pinched. This means the leaf is properly cured and matured. The too-moist cigar will make no sound. The dry cigar will crackle like a forest fire.

Burning characteristics can also be assessed by touch. Any cigar packed too tightly (even an expensive quality custom)

29

will be difficult to light, hard on the draw, prone to die. Such a cigar is strangling itself. A cigar packed too loosely will burn hot, fast and will generate too much smoke.

Other imperfections can be detected by touch, particularly such flaws as "knots" beneath wrappers. A knot is a tight bunching of filler in one spot. It acts as a plug and blocks the passage of smoke. Every cigar should be tested for knots before being put to a match. A good tobacconist will replace a knotted cigar without argument.

Of wines and cigars

Since comparisons abound between vintage wines (or other beverages) and cigars, a question arises: are there such things as compatible matings?

Yes. Here are six:

After a meal of solid food and rich sauces: some icy Williams pear brandy from Switzerland and a mild American custom claro. Any shape will do.

Late in the evening: a 1945 vintage port and a deep-flavored Brazilian cigar; one of the lighter coronas is best.

After a banquet: syrupy, spicy Drambuie and a rich Cameroon corona.

When simply smoking and drinking, without food: Canadian whiskey neat and one of the short Dutch imports generally sold only in good American shops.

For succor on a muggy, hot afternoon: subtle Italian Galliano (over crushed ice with a lime-peel twist) and a corona maduro colorado from Nicaragua.

On a chill afternoon, to bring on inner warmth: the sweet Kahlua coffee liqueur from Mexico and a pencil-thin panatela of strong and fortifying leaf from the same country.

Mark Twain once said he was deprived of cigars until he was eight years old but made up for that hardship with heavy smoking later.

Twain is said to have had his own favorite combination of tobacco and strong drink. It wasn't sophisticated, but it was as American as his books.

The ideal drink with a fine cigar, Twain claimed, was beer.

30

3

The storage problem

If not heat, surely humidity

An English automobile manufacturing executive (name with-
held by his tobacconist) was posted to Brazil in the winter
of 1968. There he was to build an organization which would
market his company's cars in competition with German and
Japanese imports.

When he flew from London with his wife early that
December he brought with him three boxes of his favorite
panatelas.

A week later, however, when he and his wife were moving
into their new apartment in Rio de Janeiro, he could find
only two.

Had the missing box been stolen by baggage handlers?
Lost in customs? No matter. Cigars are plentiful in Brazil.
Still, he regretted losing his own cigars. They had been especially selected for him and aged to his particular taste for more
than a year in his tobacconist's shop.

Over a year later, the man and his wife were preparing to
return to England for a Christmas visit. As the woman took their
heavy clothing from a cedar chest and shook free the mothballs,
the lost box of cigars fell out.

The cigars inside were dry, discolored specimens. They reeked of camphor. They were unsmokable.

"Throw the beastly things out," said the wife.

"I should," the man answered. "But they were really good cigars. And I think that particular kind has been discontinued. I wonder . . . ? What if . . . ?"

In London he took them to his tobacco shop. "Is there any way these can be revived? I know it's hardly worth trying. But the principle of the thing is important, you know."

The tobacconist held one to his nose. He winced but he nodded. Yes. Being English, he understood the appeal to this particular principle.

First he ventilated the smelly cigars for a week in a circulating-air chamber to permit them to "breathe," as is said in the trade. Next he placed them in a humidor by themselves at the proper temperature and humidity. Then, when the camphor smell had worn off, he placed them in his huge storage room (in effect, an oversized humidor) and let them rest.

Six months later the auto firm executive received his cigars in Rio by air express. They were firm again. They were properly moist. Their color had returned. And, except for a slight chemical taste and aroma when smoked down to too small a butt, they were nearly perfect.

An enclosed note read: "Cost of air freight is 10 shillings and 6 pence. No charge for resuscitation of the panatelas. For the future, sir, we suggest you either pack more carefully or take your wife's advice. Not even for a principle is this worth doing twice "

A twofold moral

The moral of the above story is twofold. One, a good cigar is no better than the place in which it is stored. Two, proper storage can sometimes make a sick cigar well.

It will surely make a good cigar taste better. Comparison to the vintner's art is again inevitable. Cultivating the grapes, fermenting the wine and finally bottling it are complicated and demanding processes. No good vintner would store his bottles carelessly after so much delicate attention.

By the same token, growing tobacco, aging and curing it; and manufacturing the cigars, are also complicated and demanding processes. No connoisseur would store his cigars carelessly. Cigars, like wine, can spoil. Yet smokers all too often put their cigars away with no more care than they waste on their socks.

It should be made clear that we speak of the individual smoker's storage problems in this chapter. The tobacconist's requirements differ, if only because of his inventory volume.

The individual smoker must nonetheless be concerned with his tobacco man's storage facilities and capabilities. If a dealer is indifferent or careless, the cigars he sells may be in poor condition. Any tobacco shop can be assessed quickly. If a smoker doesn't like what he sees and hears, he should switch shops. If he is satisfied, he should assume that his retailer is selling "fresh" cigars until such time as proven otherwise.

The peak of smoking freshness will vary from one cigar type to another.

Some cigars remain fresh for only a few weeks after arrival at the tobacconist's. Then they begin a process sometimes called "the fourth stage of fermentation." If not smoked when fresh, such cigars should be "put to rest" for another year until this process is finished.

Freshness can be affected by a tobacco shop's storage techniques. For example, a careless dealer is apt to keep his cigars warm, but too much heat in a cigar display case can disastrously dehydrate the contents.

Smoker preferences also enter the question. What is a fresh cigar to one person may be "green" to another and perhaps even stale to a third. Some smokers ask their dealers to notify them immediately whenever new cigars arrive, but others feel these same cigars are unappetizing until they have had shelf time in which to recuperate from traveling conditions.

To repeat a thought stated frequently before: each smoker must establish his own taste standards by trial and error.

The smoker's responsibility

Once he has purchased cigars assumed to be fresh, it is the

33

smoker's responsibility to keep them fresh until they are smoked. Just how long cigars can be kept before taste and aroma deteriorate is a moot point.

Consider some Caribbean products. Some will keep for 25 years, others will keep but three. Some expensive cigars will stay at peak only a few months. Some cheap cigars are "good" for years, being so bad to begin with that little can happen to them to make them worse.

One rule of thumb: a good custom quality-grade cigar can usually be stored for about a year.

Another rule of thumb: the one-cigar-per-day man should not buy five boxes just because they happen to represent a bargain. Some of those he smokes last are likely to have become losers.

It should be noted that truly bad home storage, though possible, is difficult to accomplish. Actually to ruin his supply, a smoker would almost have to set out purposely with destruction on his mind. Tropic and desert climates offer special problems with temperature and humidity extremes, but storage is easy in the temperate areas if only some care is exercised. Few cigars are ever ruined to the point of total loss merely by poor or careless treatment. The cigars in the Englishman's mothballs were an exception.

Carelessness and improper storage *do* exact their price, however. This is regrettable since no cigar has to suffer premature deterioration after purchase if it was a quality cigar in good condition to start with. Actually, storage (or "keeping") is quite simple.

There are only two basic rules, and the smoker who follows them with reasonable diligence can keep his cigars in ideal smoking condition during their full life expectancy. They will stand up under minor violations.

1. Be concerned with temperature and humidity levels. Too much heat or too little heat, too much moisture or too little moisture, are about the only things that can seriously erode a cigar's smoking characteristics.

2. Choose a storage spot away from radiators and air conditioners. For a container, a special cigar humidor is preferable to anything else. Note: a wooden cigar box will often serve as

34

an excellent substitute. So will a glass jar, but humidors are still best.

Regarding rule No. 1 concerning proper temperature and humidity:

The chapter on choosing cigars says that one mark of a good tobacconist is the temperature and humidity of his storage areas. To restate these data: optimum storage temperature lies somewhere between the mid-60s and mid-70s. The ideal humidity range is from 60 to 67 percent. More precise numbers than these do not exist.

Happily, the figures are not that critical for the smoker who stocks but a small number of cigars to be smoked within a short while, say, a month. His cigars will remain in fine shape until used as long as the fluctuations in temperature and humidity are not too wide.

Temperature and humidity

There will be such fluctuations. Temperatures in houses and apartments vary from summer to winter. Humidity will go up to 90 percent on one summer day, down to 40 percent on another. Few American smokers, even those who consider themselves connoisseurs, are anxious to become involved with or pay for large humidors and vaults or temperature and humidity control equipment. A cool dry cellar or an ordinary shelf in a cool dry corner is sufficient, as long as the cigars are kept in a relatively airtight humidor.

Regarding rule No. 2 concerning proper storage places:

The home humidor is a relatively modern development. Until about 1900, smokers (who were mostly men) kept cigars in cans, shoe boxes, even cookie tins.

Eighteenth- and 19th-century Hollanders and Frenchmen liked to have their cigars displayed in porcelain stands with holes in which each cigar stood upright, rather like pipes in a pipe rack. The visual effect was that of bunches of fat brown stalks. These stands or "urns" represented *art nouveau* then, are collector's items now, and tend to be hard on tobacco at any time.

The home humidor is still the best storage place for the small cigar collection, say, 200 of several different types. This may seem a large number, but to the five-cigar-per-day smoker it represents six weeks' supply. Incidentally, many connoisseurs insist that smoking more than five cigars daily is nicotine gluttony.

Good starter humidors holding even fewer cigars can be purchased for as little as $10. Such containers generally feature tight-fitting hinged lids or slip-on covers and come equipped with a humidifying element inside. (The simplest and most effective small humidor element consists of a glass tube, open at each end, with a sponge inside that can be moistened.)

The finest humidors are made of wood, and the finest humidor wood is cedar. If the humidor itself is not entirely made of cedar, it should at least be lined with cedar for the best service to the cigars filling it.

Many tobacco specialty shops sell jumbo humidors with 500-cigar capacities. Some are quite ornate and sometimes cost several thousand dollars. All of the big ones serve two functions. One, they hold the cigars ready for immediate smoking. Two, they store cigars that are "resting" till reaching peak freshness.

As mentioned earlier, the most inexpensive (but still effective) humidor is the cedar box in which quality cigars are usually packed. The cardboard boxes used commonly today to hold cheaper brands will not do. The paper laminations "leak" and the cigars inside eventually suffer. Simple glass-tube-and-sponge humidifiers are available for use inside cigar boxes. They are manufactured in most cigar sizes and fit the place of a single cigar.

Some expensive cigars are packaged in individual glass or aluminum tubes sealed with corks or screw-on caps. These individual tubes must be considered simple humidors. They do a fine job of preserving each cigar in a suitable environment regardless of temperature and humidity changes outside.

The cellophane wrapper found on so many American-made products represents still another humidor of sorts. These wrappers definitely retard the drying-out process but by no means offer a lasting protection. Cellophane has several disadvantages, in fact. Once a cigar inside the cellophane loses its moisture, restoring it to good condition is virtually impossible without breaking the seal and unwrapping it.

Humidors not only preserve the good condition of fresh cigars, they also are helpful in restoring sick cigars. The incident of the English automobile executive is a classic, if atypical example. It is true, however. A long rest inside a well-tempered humidor will bring brittle and stale cigars back close to their original elasticity and freshness. The process may take as long as six months, but it can work.

Institutional advice

The Cigar Institute of America at 1270 Avenue of the Americas, New York, New York 10020 offers some important advice on keeping small private stocks of cigars fresh in the home or apartment. The smokers' CIA is an industry-wide organization embracing manufacturers, growers, distributors and related concerns. One of its functions is consumer service and one of its statements is particularly comforting: "If you use up your box of 50 cigars in a few weeks, and assuming they were in good condition when you bought them (if they weren't, you had better have a talk with your dealer), and assuming you don't keep them near a radiator, you should never have a problem of humidification."

Other CIA statements debunk some commonly held notions.

On refrigeration, for example: "Keeping cigars in your refrigerator is definitely not the answer to humidification, particularly because cigars have a definite tendency to pick up odors. For this reason, by no means succumb to the old theory of maintaining freshness by inserting an apple or potato slice in your cigar box. And don't keep lighter fluid, chewing gum, candy, et cetera, in the same container with cigars."

On building bricks: "Use of wet building bricks or wet rolled-up newspapers as substitutes for a humidification device should definitely be avoided. Such makeshifts may ·moisten cigars but they contain certain organic matter which rapidly becomes moldy and creates an odor and may draw cockroaches."

On the quality of moisture: "Cool moisture is best. It is dangerous to evaporate water by means of heat where cigars are kept. Heat about 70 degrees may hatch out worms. Eggs of the tobacco beetle are occasionally present in cigar tobacco."

On reconditioning: "Forced reconditioning of dry cigars by means of steam is decidedly detrimental, as this will loosen and blister cigar wrappers and cause mold."

Pre-Columbian Indians had no known temperature or humidity problems. Except for tobacco prepared and kept for ceremonial purposes, they generally fabricated their *zikars* on the spot and smoked them as needed.

Prolonged storage is a problem created by the western men who first smoked tobacco. It has been nagging smokers ever since and no single universal solution has ever been devised. Once again, the smoker must play it by ear.

38

In humid climates, for example, moisture is ruinous. Cigars won't light; they gather mildew. The Dutch have licked this problem nicely in their drizzly, wet country by "glass storage." The manufacturers pack certain expensive cigars in airtight glass or ceramic humidors that seal the contents against moisture damage. Thrifty Dutch who buy cheaper brands supply their own canning jars with rubber seals in the lids.

Cigars acquiring mold or "bloom" still have a chance for survival. Wipe the bloom from each cigar with a soft clean brush, then store in a tight-lidded humidor in some dry spot for three months or longer. Prolonged dry rest may restore such cigars to smokable condition. Unfortunately, however, there is no way to tell that this will happen. Three months is often just enough time to produce only cigar-shaped piles of rot.

Dryness is an annoyance of the other extreme.

The late Vice-President John Nance Garner solved that problem in his own inventive way. This thorny Texan who served under President Franklin D. Roosevelt is said to have frequently carried his cigars inside the Stetson on his head because he considered this the only way to keep them moist outdoors in the torturous dry Panhandle heat.

4

Lighting up

"A good cigar is a smoke."

"A woman is only a woman," Rudyard Kipling wrote in *The Betrothed,* "but a good cigar is a smoke." The rarely enigmatic Mr. Kipling might in this instance have posed a problem for future English literature classes trying to figure out just what he meant. Nonetheless, there is no doubt that the cigar held an exalted position in his set of values. He was fond of sending boxes of his favorite brand to friends. Once, in a reversal of form, he sent a box of evil-smelling Italian cheroots to a critic who had written an unfavorable review of one of his books.

As did many of the more affluent men around the turn of the century, Kipling had his cigars embossed with his initials on each band and on the label of the box. Boxes of such private-brand cigars were often sent to the smoker's favorite restaurants and clubs for his exclusive use. Such places as Rector's and Delmonico's in New York maintained giant-sized humidors that held hundreds of boxes of private-brand cigars. This gracious practice is still followed, though to a lesser degree, at such places as the Knickerbocker Club and the Racquet and Tennis Club.

Money has rarely stood in the way of the man who really

wanted a fine smoke. The Rothchilds of Paris used to order 40,000 Henry Clay Sobranos at a time. A shipment of cigars for Napoleon III, each tipped in gold and embossed with the imperial "N," cost an estimated $120,000.

Who is to say, however, that the $2 stogies Diamond Jim Brady used to smoke tasted any better to him than the 2-cents-a-handful "loose twists" did to the Irish gandy-dancers working on those same railroad tracks over which Brady rode in his private carriage? The point is, rich or poor, men have found one of the great pleasures in life to be cigar smoking.

The man who has tried occasionally smoking cigars and claims he doesn't like them, can usually discover a reason for the dislike. Like skiing, cooking or building a house, cigar smoking should be done in the proper manner. When ineptly approached, the results can be disastrous (as witness the man who lights a cigar from the wrong end and has the wrapper leaf unravel in his mouth).

The best way to test the quality of a cigar, it has been said all too many times, is by smoking it. And to get a proper smoke from a cigar, considerable care must be taken before it is ever lighted. Cigars are fragile; they should be handled with delicacy and style.

To begin with, when a closed cigar box is opened (generally by splitting the paper trimmings on the sides with a razor blade or a penknife), caution must be exercised to prevent scratching into the cigars on the top layer. It is also a good idea to use a wooden spill of some sort when removing the first cigar from the box, thus avoiding unnecessary squeezing. This is more of a problem than many people realize, since most boxes are tightly packed. If a spill is not available, the first cigar can be removed by gently pressing the rounded end. The pressure raises the other end and enables the smoker to remove the cigar without damaging it. (A spill is simply a lever, usually of wood, used for lifting tightly packed cigars.)

Preparation counts

Preparation of the cigar prior to smoking is a good part of the battle. An incision must be made in the head end (or cap, as it is sometimes called) before the cigar is lit. This is done to provide an adequate draft, allowing the oil in the tobacco leaf to burn steadily.

The best implement for opening the head is a cigar cutter that produces either a straight line or V-shaped incision. Patented cigar cutters can range in price anywhere from 35 cents at the corner tobacconist to the $2,000 diamond-encrusted gold device once used by J. P. Morgan. Morgan's cutter was made in the form of a golden dog. When the dog's tail was raised, its mouth opened and the end of the cigar could be inserted in it. Then the tail would be snapped down, the dog would take his bite, as it were, and the cigar was tipped with precision. (The diamonds, incidentally, formed the dog's collar.)

For smokers unwilling (and unable) to buy $2,000 gadgets, a small sharp penknife will do. For best results, hold the knife in one hand, moving the cigar against the point while pressing lightly behind the head of the cigar with one thumb. The V-shape should be cut in two distinct downward movements.

41

The impatient man can simply bite the tip off, or, with an exceptionally dry cigar, squeeze the head end between thumb and forefinger until a split appears. Whatever method is used, the tip should be lightly moistened before cutting to avoid possible cracking of the wrapper leaf. Some aficionados, incidentally, recommend running the tip of the tongue down the entire length of the cigar, but (except when smoking exceptionally dry cigars) this is generally considered poor form.

Under no circumstances should the tip of a cigar ever be *pierced*. The reason is basic: piercing produces a concentrated, round, pipelike draft. The fire will burn most intensely right at the opposite end of the "flue" thus created. The surrounding fire, however, will die out from lack of oxygen. Most complaints received by tobacconists deal with unevenly burning cigars. Invariably, such cigars turn out to have been pierced rather than cut.

As one British authority on smoking has put it, "Show me a man who pierces a cigar with the end of a match and I'll show you a barbarian, and probably an American barbarian at that."

Once the cigar has been tipped, is it then ready for lighting?

No. There is still the band to contend with.

Here the smoker has his choice: the custom of Continental cigar smokers is to remove the band immediately. Other smokers prefer to leave it on, a completely acceptable practice.

If the band *is* to be removed, it must be done carefully to avoid tearing the wrapper leaf. The most efficient method: lightly squeeze the cigar by the band with the thumb and forefinger of the right hand so that the largest part of the band (usually at the front with the brand name on it) can be pulled downward, off the cigar.

Now, at last, the cigar is ready for lighting.

The primary objective of course is to light it in such a manner that it burns slowly and evenly throughout the life of the cigar.

Starring Leslie Caron

42

One scene in the film "Gigi" shows Leslie Caron learning how to light a man's cigar properly, as part of her training in the art of being a "professional companion." The connoisseur who insists upon lighting his own would scoff at such heresy.

For the man without a Leslie Caron, one common method of cigar lighting is as follows: the flame should be held slightly below, but not touching, the butt end of the cigar. Draw evenly and, as the cigar ignites, rotate it slowly with the other hand so that the flame touches every part of the end. When it appears to be lighted, remove it from the mouth and blow gently on the burning end to be sure it is fully and evenly lit. If it is not, apply the flame again.

This is simple and widely practiced, but it is not the best method. The man who truly knows and loves cigars is more patient in lighting up. What he achieves is a light that warms his cigar properly, accelerating the burning gradually without overheating the tip or producing the gusts of harsh smoke characteristic of other lighting methods. The following requires time and patience, but try it if you do not already light cigars in this manner. The effort is worthwhile.

Begin with three wooden matches. Two *may* do, but three are usually required.

Strike one.

Hold the tuck (lighting end) of the cigar between thumb and forefinger just above the tip of the flame, the point at which the greatest heat is generated. Roll the cigar back and forth between your fingers, evenly singeing the exposed filler ends. Repeat the same procedure with the second and, if necessary, the third match. This gently drives the water from the tobacco and raises it to the combustion point. (All cigars contain some moisture, which renders them fire-resistant to some degree. Ten to 12 percent is the optimum moisture level.)

After some seconds of this slow heating and turning, a gush of bluish flame will shoot from the foot of the cigar. The moisture has been driven out and the natural tobacco oils are now at ignition temperature. The cigar is evenly lit and burning at comfortably low temperatures.

Note: the cigar has "lit itself" in a sense. At no time has it been in the mouth.

As mentioned before, there are two sides to the question of relighting a cigar once it has gone out. Arguments on either aspect tend to become specious. (Example: One noted Dutch manufacturer insists that no cigar that has gone out should *ever* be relighted because a fresh one is always better and, in his words, ". . . It just doesn't cost that much. Any man who can afford one cigar can always afford another.") Winston Churchill, on the other hand, was constantly relighting "dead" cigars. Reportedly he once explained to United States Secretary of State Cordell Hull that he actually preferred them that way. "They're gamier after they've been resurrected a bit," he said.

They certainly are.

43

Clearing the air

Actually, any cigar that is relighted immediately after it goes out will taste little different (and not unpleasantly so) from the way it did before. If it is allowed to cool off, however, it is likely to taste bitter. When relighting a cigar, always squeeze the end between thumb and forefinger to remove any dead ash that may remain just inside the unburned portion of wrapper leaf.

The old-timers who claim cigars should be lighted only with a wooden match are quite correct. Bookmatches or gas lighters will not (repeat, not) do just as well. Cigar or cigarette lighters that use lighter fluid are also to be avoided. The fumes from all lighters will impregnate the tobacco leaf, imparting a noxious odor to it.

Never stub out a cigar. Just lay it on an ashtray and it will quickly go out of its own accord. Stubbing out a cigar increases the smoldering area and causes an unpleasant smell.

It is a good idea, incidentally, to throw out old butts as soon as possible. It is the smell of discarded butts, not the aroma of a lighted cigar, that some people find objectionable.

There is even an answer to that cantankerous housewife who insists loudly (and inaccurately) that "I can't *stand* the smell of cigars, because it gets in the curtains and stays there." This is sheer balderdash, of course, but the woman can be mollified by burning a large candle whenever a cigar is being smoked. Somehow it manages to clear the air of any trace of tobacco aroma.

Happily, such women are few in number. In a recent survey by Robert Boate Foster, the English public opinion survey expert, the words most women associated with cigar smoking were "virile," "wealthy" and "sophisticated."

As a matter of fact, there is a well-known toilet preparation for men called "Tabac" which uses a tobacco base. There is also a fabric shade in the fashion world—a rich, dark brown —that is known as Tobacco Brown.

Pointers for pleasure

Here, in capsule form, are a few points (some repeated) which will enhance the undeniable pleasure to be derived from smoking fine cigars:

1. Reminder: take a few extra seconds to light your cigar carefully and evenly, so that it will not burn down the side.

2. Puff slowly. A short pause between puffs will enable you to enjoy the full fragrance of the cigar.

3. Always insist upon a fresh cigar from the retailer. A cigar that is not "factory fresh" will have lost some of its flavor. An inexpensive humidor, properly maintained, will further insure freshness.

4. Remember: cigars that are regular in size, shape and color are more likely to smoke consistently, each as good as the last. Regularity of appearance denotes, at the very least, care in selection and pride in workmanship.

5. Buy your cigars well in advance of smoking them. Up to a point, age will improve most varieties. They can be smoked with pleasure when they are much older.

6. Carry cigars in a leather or plastic cigar case to protect them from crushing. When carried in the breast pocket of a suit, cigars should always be placed with the head end down. (Governor Alfred E. Smith of New York reputedly carried his cigars tucked into the tops of his gartered socks, rather like a Scotsman carrying a dirk. It is not, however, a recommended practice.)

7. Try to maintain about an inch of ash on the point of the cigar, a practice that will provide a much cooler smoke.

8. Don't keep a cigar in your mouth when you talk. This usually dislodges the ash, makes it necessary to bite into the cigar to hold it and, besides, will make your conversation unintelligible.

For those who have yet to discover the delights of cigar smoking, it is tobacco enjoyment in its finest form. More than 15 million men have discovered and enriched their lives with the cigar's aroma and intriguing flavor. The proper introduction to smoking cigars can result in a lifetime friendship and its cultivation deserves time and thought. Somewhere there is the right cigar for every potential cigar smoker. It pays to keep searching, for it has been said that a man's road can never be completely without brightness as long as there is one cigar in his pocket; nor can he ever be truly alone, for there is companionship in cigars. The smoke of a good cigar is a great thing. So many of man's troubles go up in it.

5

The art of smoking

And some people who smoke

The worlds of art and tobacco are not unrelated, far apart though they may seem at first glance. Certainly the artist has played a large part in the history of pipe smoking; he created the intricately carved designs so cherished by collectors. By the same token, the cigar store Indians, the flamboyantly designed cigar-box labels and the individualistic cigar bands represent their own unique art form.

Cigar store Indians are rare collector's items today, but they once commonly graced the front of virtually every tobacco store in every town in this country. The first in America may have been the one in front of D. H. McAlpine's shop in New York City, which was established in 1840.

At that, America was far behind England. Carved figures holding cigars were seen as early as the middle 1600s in London. Usually the wooden figure represented an African chieftain wearing a headdress of tobacco leaves. By the 18th century, the African was more often replaced by a gilded Punch or a kilted Highlander. The Indian did not appear for another 100 years or so and he didn't really last too long. It is estimated that there are only 3,000 wooden cigar store Indians surviving today, mostly in private or museum collections of Americana.

One of the finest examples of wooden Indian art stands in the foyer of the Cattleman's Restaurant in New York City. The Palmer House in Chicago has another. An exquisite one is owned by the New York Museum of Natural History. Oddly, one of the really great examples perished when the Shepheard's Hotel in Cairo burned to the ground.

Say "cigar art" to most people, and they will usually assume you are talking about cigar bands. True artistic touches, however, appeared more often on cigar boxes and cigar-box labels than on the bands. Cigar boxes developed from utilitarian containers into works of art decorated with colorful lithographs. In the Golden Era of cigars (late 19th and 20th centuries) manufacturers went to great lengths to produce labels that would catch the smoker's eye.

The finest color lithographers of the day were employed to create new designs. Before embossing became common in the 1880s, some lithographers used as many as 22 different stones for a single label. The designers were given full freedom, and they took full advantage of it. Voluptuous, short-skirted ladies made their appearance on cigar boxes by the hundreds. At the time they were considered "naughty." Today they would be called "camp." In any case, no statistics survive to indicate what effect they had on sales.

47

For quite some time labels dripped with symbolic nicotinic borders, flowers of the garden and flowers of womanhood, but eventually the "pitch" changed and more masculine themes were adopted. Hundreds of new brand names appeared in the United States reflecting the thinking of the times. There was THE NABOB, CLUBMAN'S FAVORITE, SILVERTIP, GOLDEN TIMES and HIGHLANDER. Some brand names, all of which were well known in their times, would seem strange today: THE CHICAGO FANNY, CHARMS, AESTHETIC, DAISY, MY TWO GIRLS, DEERSLAYER, SPREAD EAGLE, TELEPHONE, NIGHTCAP, ULTIMATUM, SNOW FLAKE, BULLY, FOUR MONKS, OLD LAVENDER, TOM DICK AND HARRY, GOLDEN CHARM and IROQUOIS.

If prizes were given for such inventiveness, a top one would have to go to the manufacturer who wanted to emphasize the fact that his cigars were handmade. The cigar-box label merely showed a man's extended hand, with the word "made" printed across the palm. At the time it was considered frightfully clever.

Collector's items

Cigar bands have been collector's items ever since they were first introduced. But when were they introduced? There are several stories answering this question, one probably as good as another.

One legend has it that the ladies of the Court of Spain, following the pattern set by their men, quickly picked up the habit of cigar smoking. At that time it was the height of fashion to participate in anything remotely suggesting the fabulous New World. According to legend, the Duchess of Alba first wrapped a wide band of paper around the lower part of the cigar so as not to stain her delicate fingers. Thus the duchess seems to have created the first cigar band.

A less romantic version has it that the custom started among English dandies of the mid-1800s who were afraid of soiling the white gloves so popular during that era.

Probably closer to the fact is the report ascribing the invention of the cigar band to one Mynheer Bock, a Dutchman who in 1854 became one of the first Europeans to cultivate a Caribbean tobacco plantation. Bock (who, according to one source was named Gustave, according to another H. Anton) reputedly noticed that he would occasionally find a poor-quality cigar in a box that was supposed to contain his own brand. Realizing that someone was removing his product and palming off a poor cigar in its place, he designed a small paper circlet that he attached to his cigars to prevent counterfeiting.

The band is now in general use, of course, and has developed a fascination all its own. Zino Davidoff in his fine book, *The Connoisseur's Book of the Cigar* writes: "It has attained the level of a precious object. I have seen some sumptuous bands designed by great painters. I have also seen them decorated with gold, ostrich plumes, diamond fragments. Fantastic prices have been received for some collections containing thousands of examples."

48

It was Gustave (or H. Anton) Bock, by the way, who wrote the first book called *Art of Smoking the Cigar.* In that small volume he tells of inventing the cigar band.

Today cigar bands bear their own legends. King Farouk of Egypt reportedly marched into a Geneva cigar store and said, "I have 15,000 cigar bands for double coronas in reserve. Can you furnish me with the right cigars?" And would you believe that Ernest Hemingway once presented Ava Gardner with a cigar band as a souvenir of their first meeting?

One of the cigar bands most prized by today's collectors is the one personally decorated by Edward VII of England, who drew up a design showing three white plumes and then had an artist render it in detail.

It was Edward VII, incidentally, who is credited with one of the better-known quotations in the smoking world. As Prince of Wales, he had suffered under the ban issued by his mother, Queen Victoria, against smoking cigars in her presence. On the day he assumed the throne, one of his first edicts was "Gentlemen, you may smoke."

To this day, Edward, Duke of Windsor, is an avid cigar smoker who prefers double coronas.

49

The unorthodox Morgan

Somewhat more unorthodox in matters of preference was J. P. Morgan. When he was in a hurry he smoked a small five-inch Regalia de Morgan. When he was in less of a hurry, however, he would choose a six-and-a-half-inch selecto. Only when he had full leisure would he turn to his favorite, an eight-inch torpedo-shaped Kohinoor.

Eight inches, of course, is not exactly giant size. When Samuel Gompers was ordered by his physician to cut his cigar consumption to one a day, the labor leader (once a cigar maker) began turning out a huge 12-incher each morning. John Wayne also has special oversized cigars made to enhance his "he-man" image. They are impressive to look at but, according to the movie star himself, rather bitter to the tongue.

Wayne is only one of many top stars who prefers cigars, and occasionally they have served to help create screen char-

Cigar Store "Indians"

acter. Remember Edward G. Robinson and his gangster roles? In 1949 he was named Cigar Smoker of the Year by American importers. Off the screen Robinson is a heavy cigar smoker but, unlike the Robinson of the movies, he carefully abstains from chewing them.

Other Hollywood cigar smokers include Charles Coburn and Clark Gable (now dead) and Jack Warner and Orson Welles. Perhaps the best-known, however, is Groucho Marx. When his wife threatened to divorce him if he did not give up cigars, his reputed answer was: "Well, I hope we can remain good friends, my dear."

Not all women have been so truculent when it comes to cigars. Queen Victoria's distaste for them notwithstanding, cigar smoking was popular among the ladies in royal courts throughout Europe for more than 100 years. One portrait of Catherine the Great shows her smoking a cigar. As author George Sand wrote: "The cigar numbs sorrow and fills the solitary hours with a million gracious images." She herself was rarely without a cigar; actresses impersonating her have invariably used one as a prop.

Screen stars like Greta Garbo, Anne Baxter and Joan Fontaine buttressed the trend in Hollywood years ago. Today such actresses as Elizabeth Taylor, Mia Farrow, Julie Christie, Sara Miles, Natalie Wood, Lauren Bacall, Edie Adams, Renata Boeck, Carol Lynley and Piper Laurie puff cigars. Do you want more names? Consider Keely Smith, Lena Horne, Marlene Dietrich, Gloria Vanderbilt, Mrs. Sargent Shriver.

Lady cigar smokers reside elsewhere besides the United States. Britain's Princess Margaret and Monaco's Princess Grace head the overseas list; the Maharanee of Baroda is another cigar devotee.

Happily, most men are not as intransigent as General Pierre Gallifet, a French officer noted for his reactionary resistance to all change. He forbade any woman to smoke cigars in his presence. Unfeminine, he said. When dining at a friend's home one night General Gallifet observed a young woman lighting a slim cigar. He walked over to her, took her by the arm and said, "Come, my dear! *Allons pisser!*"

Feminism might not have bothered Ulysses S. Grant, who

52

averaged more than 750 cigars a month when he was President. He was too busy smoking to have really cared. The humorist Mark Twain was equally indifferent to such "ideology." He bought his cigars by the barrel and smoked them incessantly. When asked how he remained so spry after he was 70, he replied, "I owe it to the fact that I never smoke more than one cigar at a time."

To the names of Churchill (who is said to have smoked more than 300,000 cigars in his lifetime), Freud (who once said, "My cigar is not a symbol. It is only a cigar."), astronaut John Glenn and composer Franz Liszt, add the name of Don Rodrigo de Xeres. According to the logbook of Vicente Pinzon, Don Rodrigo was the first European to smoke a cigar. The date, as recorded in Pinzon's log: October 28, 1492.

Perhaps one other name should be added to the Cigar Smoker's Hall of Fame: Columnist Hal Boyle. In a column for the Associated Press Boyle once advanced the sacrilegious proposition that a cigar, not a dog, is man's best friend.

Wrote Boyle: "A cigar does not sit up and beg, but on the other hand it does not leave hairs on the sofa or track mud in on the rug. A cigar does not wag its tail in a friendly manner, but neither does it have to be fed or taken for walks morning and evening in all kinds of weather. A cigar cannot be taught to fetch your slippers; however, a cigar smoker can always teach his wife to do that."

53

Four comics who enjoy a good smoke: Left, Alan King; above, left to right, Milton Berle, Joey Bishop and Jimmy Durante.

6

In the beginning

A history of smoking, tobacco and cigars

In the beginning, according to the Susquehanna Indians of Pennsylvania, men ate only the flesh of animals and knew nothing of planting crops. One day three braves journeyed far from their village to hunt. Their eyes were sharp and their bows true, and on their first day they killed a fine deer.

As they roasted the rich meat that evening, there appeared on a nearby hillside a lovely maiden in a glow of light—a wood nymph. Though their hearts were filled with fear and apprehension, the men stood fast. One said, "This spirit is hungry. She has been drawn to us by the smell of our cooking meat. Let us share our meal with her. She will be pleased and bring us no harm."

And so speaking, he placed tender cuts and meaty ribs on a large, rain-scrubbed stone near the figure.

The warrior's judgment was as accurate as his bow. The wood nymph ate and was grateful. She called to the watching men: "Your kindness shows you love and respect your gods. Such goodness should not go unrecognized. When thirteen moons have gone, return to this spot where I have eaten. Here your reward will await you, oh good men."

In the beginning

After the 13th moon, the three returned as instructed. They found maize, beans and tobacco sprouting close to the stone upon which they had placed the cooked venison.

They had never seen such plants, but they knew they came from the gods and therefore required care and nurturing. The three remained, pampering and watering the fragile shoots. The shoots grew and bore fruit. After the harvest, the three braves brought the crops back to their people, who marveled at the maize and beans and loved the fragrant smell and fine taste of the burning tobacco.

Man has enjoyed the gifts of maize, beans and tobacco since that day. But of the three, he enjoys tobacco most.

A historical accident

No one can identify the first smokers with certainty. Undoubtedly the first smoking experiences were what the American educator and philosopher Will Durant might call a "historical accident," somewhat akin to Sir Alexander Fleming's experience on finding mold on his luncheon bread one day in 1929—a happenstance that led to the discovery of penicillin.

The first smoker was probably a prehistoric man who inhaled the fumes of his resinous wood fire quite accidentally and found them pleasant. Later, perhaps, he might have thrown additional ingredients into subsequent fires (herbs, various woods, seaweed) to create varieties of smoke and odors.

About 600 B.C., the Celts of Britain had learned to mine and work iron, and among the things they fashioned were pipes, massive smoking machines heavy enough to serve as clubs. These crude pipes were used for smoking mixtures of indigenous spices, woods and greens.

The Egyptians of antiquity burned incense, myrrh and other aromatics in temples and closed chambers, inhaling the odors. This, too, was a form of smoking. Hieroglyphics in the tomb of Pharaoh Tutankhamen, the 18th-dynasty ruler of Egypt around 1350 B.C., depict incense burning and inhaling. Incense pellets were found inside the tomb when it was opened in 1922.

In the fifth century B.C., the Roman historian Herodotus

wrote of the Scythians (who lived in what is today the southern area of the Soviet Union) having "knowledge of a tree bearing strange fruit. . . . When they cast it [the fruit] upon fires 'round which they sit . . . by mere smell of the fumes . . they grow drunk. They jump up and begin to dance and sing."

There are remains of (and writing describing) pipes in Ireland, ancient Rome, China and Africa. A manuscript executed 2,000 years ago in Assyria makes the unlikely claim that the early prophets smoked pipes.

The Mayans of Mexico, however, were probably the first people to use tobacco as it is known today. The tobacco they smoked then was probably a wild, luxuriant plant, the leaves of which, tightly rolled and lighted, formed the world's first cigar.

Pleasure for the Mayans

56

The Mayan empire lasted from 1500 B.C. to about A.D. 1600. The first illustration of a man smoking appears in a relief on the Mayan temple at Palenque, Mexico, dated circa A.D. 300. The carving depicts a long tube which could be either a roll of tobacco leaves (a cigar) or a pipe. The man seems to be enjoying himself.

There is a Mayan word which reads as "zik" when transliterated into English. "Zik" is believed by German philologists to have been the noun for tobacco or smoke, and "zikar" the verb form, "to smoke." Hence the word "cigar."

The Inca civilization in Peru also knew tobacco, but it is questionable whether all men enjoyed it. Human sacrifices were part of their culture, and one of the final gifts a victim received before his heart was carved out was a roll of tobacco to smoke while contemplating "the glory of the gods and the happiness of mankind."

More closely related to present-day smoking is Columbus' report. On Monday, October 25, 1492, he wrote in his first journal about the New World: "Being at sea, about midway between Santa Maria and the large island which I named Fernandina, we met a man in a canoe . . . he had with him some dried leaves which are of high value among them, for a quantity of it was brought to me at San Salvador."

Two weeks passed before the Italian navigator actually learned that the Indians who so astounded him used the leaves in several ways to "incense themselves." In one method, they twisted the leaves into rod shapes and inserted the ends into their nostrils, lit the free ends and inhaled the smoke through the rolled bundles.

From that day on the cigar was no longer the property of the Latin American Indian.

It belonged to the world.

Odds and ends

The history of smoking, tobacco and cigars is to a great extent a collection of such odds and ends of fact and legend. The first commercial European cigar maker was one Demetrio Pela. Information about him is scanty, but he is supposed to have picked the brains of a Carib chieftain named Erioxil Panduca for the tobacco technology of New World natives and organized it to write one of the first treatises on tobacco growing. The two men later formed one of the world's first cigar companies, Panduca y Pela.

57

Pela was not the first European to roll cigars. Early in the 16th century, sailors returning to Europe intrigued the stay-at-homes with their finesse at fashioning "smoke sticks," lighting them, then sucking in the smoke.

And Pela was not the first commercial cigar and tobacco man for long. In England, tobacco shops opened faster than tobacco plants bloom under warm sun. There were 7,000 in London alone by 1617. Prices for tobacco in any form (rolls, loose leaf for pipes, snuff, chewing tobacco) reached levels never again achieved in that century: an ounce of silver for an ounce of tobacco.

Tobacco became legal tender in Virginia and in 1621 Virginia planters were paying 150 pounds of tobacco to "marriage merchants" for ". . . 60 maids of virtue, education, young and handsome," brought to the colony for sale as brides. The Virginia tobacco fields were originally seeded by John Rolfe, one of the first Jamestown colonists; the mild Virginia leaf which gives American tobacco its fine reputation today is Rolfe's.

(This farsighted man could claim one other achievement: his marriage to Pocahontas, the same Indian princess who once dissuaded her father from clubbing in the head of Captain John Smith.)

At first, and for the next 100 years, pipes were much more popular than cigars.

One reason may have been the high price of tobacco used in cigars. In Spain it was usually the well-to-do who smoked, often conspicuously, to show that they *were* well-to-do. Size was important; the larger the cigar, the more expensive the cigar, and therefore the more important the man. (This notion should not be unfamiliar. It prevails to this day.)

The Spanish cigar industry was slowly centralizing in Seville. One of the specimens turned out by a factory there was known as an "axe handle." It was a magnificent thing, a foot long and two inches in diameter at the fat belly. It weighed almost a pound.

In England, Queen Elizabeth I could not be counted among the supporters of cigars, pipes or tobacco. When Sir Walter Raleigh encouraged her to try one of his pipes, the good "Virgin Queen" agreed, then gagged and turned several colors.

Tobacco smoking survived the queen's wrath and soon became a pastime considered fit for an English gentleman for much the same reason cigars were a sign of breeding and wealth in Spain: tobacco was expensive.

Sir Walter Raleigh was one of tobacco's first public relations men. He is sometimes credited with being the man who introduced it to England. (Some historians, however, insist it was another of Elizabeth's favorites: Sir John Hawkins, the Sea Dog.) Brands of smoking tobacco and cigarettes as well as Raleigh, North Carolina, the tobacco capital of the United States, bear Raleigh's name.

A French romance

In France, tobacco's reception was more romantic. In 1559, one Jean Nicot was private secretary to Henry II of France.

The 16-year-old monarch charged Nicot with a vital mission—arrange a marriage between the king and 16-year-old Marguerite, daughter of King Sebastian of Portugal.

Nicot failed, but when he returned he brought with him tobacco plant cuttings from the private gardens of the Portuguese nobility. The gentlemen of Portugal had been smoking for decades and believed tobacco possessed some minor medicinal properties.

Now Nicot was perhaps shrewd . . . shrewd enough to cover his failure as a marriage broker with a coup in the medical field. Or perhaps he really believed what he had been told in Portugal and let his imagination run wild. Whatever the case, he came home claiming that while he had not brought a new queen for France, he *had* brought a wondrous plant named tobacco, which could cure most any ailment.

Then he set out to prove his claim. Using tobacco in several forms, he healed a chef's hacked thumb. He erased the rash from the face of a court lady. He relieved gout. He cured ulcers. He even successfully tackled a variety of "eating sores" quite likely to have been syphilis.

59

Or so he claimed.

Whether tobacco did or did not possess magical curative properties is unimportant in this context. Catherine de Médicis, who would become Henry's wife, believed it did, and this fact was enough to save Nicot's neck and popularize his name.

His failure to bring home the Portuguese bride was forgiven and/or forgotten, and in 1570 the tobacco plant was given the botanical name of *Nicotiana tabacum,* after Jean Nicot. From *Nicotiana,* of course, derives the word nicotine.

Tobacco also impressed royalty in other countries. The leaf arrived in Japan, brought in by Portuguese sailors in 1542. These men had been captured by Chinese pirates, but escaped when a typhoon hurled the Chinese ship ashore in splinters. In any case the Japanese liked the Portuguese tobacco and within 50 years people on all the Japanese home islands were smoking. The emperor himself was one of the nation's leading pipe smokers, growing his own tobacco in the royal gardens.

American sailors introduced Spanish and Caribbean cigars to Rome, a city which later became an important cigar-manu-

60

Jean Nicot presenting tobacco plant to Queen Catherine de Médicis.

facturing center. And it was in Rome that one group of sailors was tied and flogged by a mob for trying to poison the public after several men who had smoked their "samples" were sick off the docks.

The beginning

The Spanish, meanwhile, encouraged growth of a cigar industry in the Caribbean. Here, cigar making was essentially a home industry manned by hundreds of individual families working in their own houses and shops with cutting boards, sharp knives and skills developed over years. In 1698, the Spanish "nationalized" the industry, establishing a state-operated monopoly.

In New England, as in Latin America, the cigar was one of the forms of tobacco smoked by the Indians. Because its soil and climate provided such an ideal growing medium, Connecticut settlers seeded their first tobacco beds about 1630 and began growing the Colonies' best leaf. The Connecticut plant was called "shoestring" because of its narrow leaves. (Shoestring was phased out and its cultivation all but ceased in 1833; everyone was planting the more profitable Maryland Broadleaf. It was every leaf the peer of Southern tobacco, but Connecticut still grows some of the world's tastiest tobacco.)

Ironically, Connecticut with its Puritan tradition also wrote some of the harshest laws governing smoking. People under 21 were forbidden to smoke at all. Those over 21 had to find a doctor to certify that "tobacco is useful to health," obtain a smoking license and then "take tobacco" only outdoors in open fields. It was also suggested that each smoker provide himself with a bucket of water and keep it close by in the event that sparks from his cigar or pipe started a fire.

Only one witness was needed for conviction on a smoking violation.

Cigar making became a Connecticut industry in the 17th century. Cigars slowly were accepted as a form of currency and as a barter item, merchants often taking barrels of them in exchange for other goods. From Connecticut's coastal towns on Long Island Sound, American sailors picked up cigars and took them all over the world as earlier sailors had once carried Spanish cigars. Innkeepers set up cigar barrels in their common rooms and patrons were invited to help themselves. Free smoke may have been the precursor of another American custom, the "free lunch" in saloons.

During this century, wherever in the world tobacco was carried by sailors, merchants and assorted travelers, there also went with it several nicknames, the most widely used being the German "Indianisch Wundtkraut." Translation: "Indian Wonder Plant."

Tobacco's value as currency also traveled with it. When the College of William and Mary was charted in Williamsburg, Virginia, in 1693, King William III granted an income of one penny per pound on all tobacco exported from Maryland and Virginia. The money was set aside "for the education of young gentlemen."

Curious circumstances

Here are some other curious 17th-century circumstances concerning cigars and other tobacco forms (in no particular order of importance):

■ English enemies of tobacco claimed too much smoking to be fatal. One English broadside said in part, ". . . four people have died from tobacco within a week. One of them voided a bushel of soot in so doing."

■ The Chinese took notice of these warnings. Planting and/or smoking tobacco was forbidden by imperial edict and the punishment for it was an ear lopped off.

■ The Russian czar in 1634 also held tobacco in low regard, prohibited smoking and decreed: "For the first offense, smokers shall be whipped. For the second, they shall be executed."

■ English friends of tobacco followed the line of Jean Nicot and his patroness, and pipes were smoked with the regularity of vespers by students and faculty at English universities during the Great Plague (1664–1666).

Tobacco smoke was considered an immunizing agent against plague. It was told that in Hamburg, where there were thousands of cigar makers in daily contact with their tobacco, only four were plague-stricken during an epidemic. These were said to have recovered rapidly.

On a day when he passed many houses marked with the red cross which meant plague dwelt within, Samuel Pepys noted in his diary: "I was obliged to buy a roll of tobacco to smell and chew."

During the 18th century, cigars began to gain in popularity, but only slightly. Rich Spaniards still flaunted them and many other European aristocrats still claimed they were preferable to pipes, relishing the enjoyment commoners chose to ignore. On the North American mainland and the nearby Caribbean Islands, cigars were gaining a reputation of quality.

During this century, pipe smoking reached its peak in popularity, but snuff taking ran a close second. The reasons were obvious: men could "take snuff" anywhere without creating smoke clouds and the sneezy inhalant powder was "nice" enough for women of all social strata to use quite openly. Snuff was also considered the safest of all forms of using tobacco. No ignition coals or flaming splints were necessary, and it generated no sparks.

To avoid the supposed and the real dangers of cigars, it was customary in northern Europe and England for men to smoke their cigars only before fireplaces when indoors. Then any sparks or offensive fumes floated up the chimneys.

Why was the pipe always more popular than the cigar—especially when cigars would seem to possess all the advantages?

Both involve a burning process, but cigars are much simpler. A man lights one, smokes it and throws away the butt. Pipes are complex. A man must carry cleaners, scrapers and a cumbersome piece of gear—the pipe itself. Therein lies the key.

Cigar people maintain that pipes gained while cigars suffered a setback because, like weapons, pipes can be of beautiful design, something to be shown off. A cigar is a cigar, functional but forever the same basic shape and the same basic dun or olive color and forever going up in smoke, leaving only ashes.

Only one really dramatic development in smoking occurred during the 18th century, and even this was not new but only the revival of an old custom.

In the middle of the century, a few Europeans began smoking tubes of tobacco. In Brazil these tubes—which had been smoked in Latin America for years in one shape or another—were called *papelitos*.

In time, *papelitos* were to rival, then surpass, cigars and pipes in popularity. And even then the people who smoked them were calling them by the name given them today.

Cigarettes.

Worst in the world

The worst cigars ever manufactured in the world were made in the 1800s—the Italian army *segarros*. These *segarros* were offered as part of a soldier's daily rations. They varied in quality from government regime to government regime, and as the Italian military budget fattened or slimmed, so did the *segarros*. However, they were invariably awful. The worst were those made without any tobacco at all: of lime, powdered gypsum, ordinary earth, wood splinters and a length of string. Paper wrappers held these incredible products together.

Elsewhere cigar manufacture expanded production and improved quality. There were the following developments, though in no particular order of chronology or importance and often overlapping in time sequence:

■ The Caribbean cigar industry was fast becoming known as the producer of the world's finest cigars. The Spanish government ran a tight business. Wages, hours, quotas and working conditions were fixed in Madrid, rarely on a realistic basis, never on a basis compatible with the workers' needs.

Starting about 1830, however, Caribbean cigar labor began moving to Florida, the Key West area in particular. In 1868, two Cubans who were outraged at the Spanish treatment of cigar workers led a migrant group several hundred strong to Florida. They turned Tampa into "Cigar City."

As the Spanish cigar factories in the Caribbean bred labor discontent and migration, they also bred the legends of girls rolling cigars on their naked thighs to insure tight wrapper and firm packing of the filler. It was also said that they worked bare-breasted at their cutting tables because of the heat and that only the prudes among them wore blouses.

The legend persists, but legend is all it is.

■ Cigar industries sprouted like flowers of the tobacco plants themselves: in New York State and Ohio; in Jamaica and other Caribbean isles; in Europe they rose in Belgium, France and the Netherlands (especially the Netherlands); and then in Indonesia.

The great names

■ The great cigar names and styles evolved during that century: corona (round, straight, roundly blunt head); panatela (long, slender, straight, ends pointed or blunt); perfecto (fat middle, slim ends); Londres (cylindrical, one end blunt, one end round). And so on. Corona corona signifies corona brand, corona shape. There were (and still are) shape and size variations by the hundreds, but the basic configurations have remained as main criteria for the industry throughout the world.

■ Early in the 19th century in the United States there also appeared a type of cigar called the "twofer" because it sold at two for a penny. In pre-Civil War days when the purchasing power of a penny was far higher than it is today and when 50 cents was considered a fair daily wage, cigars were thought expensive even at that low price.

■ The popularity of cigars finally increased in Great Britain and Europe. Veterans of the Peninsular War in Spain (Great Britain, Portugal and Spanish guerrillas vs. Napoleonic France, 1808–1814) carried Spanish and Portuguese cigars with them throughout the Continent. The Germans in particular became great cigar lovers, a fondness for this form of tobacco that prevails there to this day.

■ The first new tools in cigar production in some 300 years appeared almost simultaneously and independently in England in the 1850s. They were wooden cigar molds or templates that were used for measuring shape. They took much of the guesswork out of handcrafting cigars, and with these molds a worker could double his manual output. There was one far-reaching effect of the molds: it moved cigar making from homes to factories. Cigar making truly became an industry.

65

■ Cigars also became forms of social expression. European feminists, the Women's Liberation people of their day, smoked cigars publicly as gestures of defiance of Victorian morality. Such women supplied cartoonists (particularly the waspish British) with subject matter that was easy to lampoon. They were shown as figures of stevedore build and wrestler face, walking with determination down crowded streets, shooing everyone from their paths with great gusts of smoke. Cigars were not for "nice" women any more than pipes or cigarettes were.

An independent woman

One 19th-century woman, mentioned earlier, did not concern herself with society's objections to cigars: Amandine Aurore Lucie Dupin of France. She was a novelist (*The Haunted Pool* and *The Master Bell Ringers* were considered her best), mistress of Frédéric Chopin, and a feminist—and better known as George Sand. She smoked cigars anywhere she pleased for the same reason she sometimes wore men's clothing: not because she was necessarily "strange," as people preferred to believe, but because she liked them.

Turning to more specific items in cigar history:

The world's most expensive cigars ever made (in terms of actual money value) were manufactured around 1900. The Britain-marketed "banker's corona" cost 12 shillings 6 pence each in 1901, or 50 pounds sterling per 100. This was a year when the pound was worth approximately $5, and $5 was considered a good week's wage. In 1901, then, one cigar that cost 12 shillings 6 pence was worth something over $3.

The smallest cigar ever manufactured is a corona shape called the Delgado which was popular for awhile in the 1800s. It was an inch and a half long. The largest, a 19-inch panatela made around the turn of the century, was never popular.

In times of financial crisis, English bankers and securities dealers made a point of smoking the expensive coronas publicly to emphasize the stability of the money market and their securities. Large cigars are still associated with "fat cats" on Wall Street.

In 1862, General Ulysses S. Grant's Union Army took Fort Donelson in Tennessee, opening the way for the capture of Nashville. The victory was an important one, and to show their gratitude, Northern cigar makers sent the general 11,000 cigars.

In 1917, United States government figures showed that there were 14,576 cigar factories operating in this country. Some were tiny one-man operations. Some were organized as subcontractors. All still employed hand-rolling methods.

The machine age

Cigarettes had been produced since 1880 in Bonsack rolling machines (named after their inventor, James Bonsack of Virginia), but cigars were still turned out by hand-pack-and-twist techniques unchanged for over four centuries. Then in

1917 Rufus L. Patterson developed a bunching and rolling machine which made 480 cigars per hour.

This contraption of slides, moving arms and levers has been modified and improved upon. Today's machines turn out 650 cigars per hour and perform just about every operation once done by deft fingers. Whatever the changes have been, however, today's machinery is still the basic Patterson idea and hardware.

One of the most famous developments in cigar history in America had nothing to do with cigars, but with politics. Thomas Marshall, Vice President under Woodrow Wilson from 1913 to 1921, was presiding over the United States Senate one day, listening to a member speak on and on about ". . . what this country needs." Said Marshall sarcastically to an aide, "What this country needs is a really good five-cent cigar."

That phrase has been a folk saying ever since.

There are still probably more than 1,000 hand producers in the country today; many of them are the small-store "mom and pop" operations in large cities. However, there are only four major factory-sized custom producers left who still craft the entire cigar from start to finish by hand.

Total United States output (all kinds, custom-made as well as mass-produced) totaled 7.8 billion in 1969.

Under Castro

Finally, current events became part of many centuries of cigar history.

When Fidel Castro liberated Cuba from the Batista regime, one of his first acts was to nationalize the two principal Cuban revenue crops—sugar and tobacco. The change was drastic—but it didn't work. It proved to be one of the cigar industry disasters of all time.

Cigar makers defected to adjacent Caribbean islands and other countries with their technology and manufacturing secrets. Dispossessed growers also left, and once outside they sued the Castro government for damages in the World Court at the Hague. Cuban cigar manufacturers opened or invested in plants in Florida, Virginia, the Philippines and the Canary Islands.

Rumor had it that growers smuggled out their best seeds, that former landowners had been torching their fields. Whether truth was part rumor or rumor part truth, in the early 1960s the quality and reputation of both Cuban leaf and finished cigars sagged like panatelas in a heavy rain.

In 1962, the John F. Kennedy administration (after considerable political abrasion between the two countries), banned the importation of Cuban leaf or cigars into the United States.

6,000 out of work

The Florida cigar industry alone had been using $22 million worth of Cuban leaf per year at this time. Within a week after the embargo, 6,000 Tampa cigar workers were out of jobs. Since that time, however, the rapidly expanding American leaf-growing and cigar-manufacturing industries have more than filled the vacuum.

68

The embargo proved a blessing, as noted in a previous chapter. As a result, United States custom cigars, traditionally of top quality, are now better than ever before. Wherever they originate, however, cigars have been one of man's pleasures for centuries, one he absolutely refuses to surrender.

An incident which took place during World War I offers classic proof.

In 1917, a merchant ship arrived in New York harbor bearing cargo from Java and Sumatra.

The arrival touched off a celebration along the waterfront. When the cargo was finally sold, the men who had underwritten the ship's voyage counted millions in profits.

The men who had crewed the ship drew enormous bonuses for hazardous duty. Well, they should have, for they had sailed without escort through the German submarine wolfpacks then cutting up Allied convoys in the Atlantic Ocean.

What was this cargo which made it so precious?

More than 33,000 bales of precious Java and Sumatra cigar-tobacco leaf, all but unobtainable in the United States since the beginning of the war.

7

One tablespoon of seed

1,500 pounds of tobacco

In the earliest descriptions of tobacco use in the New World, the cigar form is mentioned more often than any other.

These first cigars were leviathans, sometimes several inches thick at the waist. No cigars made since then approach their dimensions except perhaps those once made in the European mini-state of Andorra. These were about 30 inches long and sometimes two and a half inches thick.

There seems little need for cigars of this length today, but in pre-Columbian times in America there was. Indian planters grew plants with big leaves. Each of their "smokes" contained several leaves in one untrimmed roll.

One of the earliest pictures of this Latin leaf was given by Jan van Linschoten, who lived from 1563 to 1611 and was one of the most perceptive of the Dutch travel writers then roaming the earth. In his *Itinerario* he noted:

"There grows a kind of plant in Brazil, which the Tovoupinambaulty (an Indian tribe) call petum, and we call tabacum. Nowadays we have also got it in our gardens, but it is not as good and powerful as theirs. The savages value this fragrant weed greatly. They gather it in bunches, which they dry. Then they take four or five leaves, roll them together, and light the leaves. The smoke enables them to fast two or three days during the war."

Tobacco was a major crop then. It remains so today, still sustaining men at war.

More tobacco is raised commercially than any other non-food plant in the world; yet the plant itself (*Nicotiana tabacum*) is no longer found growing wild. That it once did grow wild is a pretty safe assumption, even if there is no evidence of it today. Nevertheless we should consider tobacco almost exclusively as a cultured crop and the high-quality cigar leaf produced today as the result of endless experimentation, centuries of seed selection and great technological advancement.

The first man who deliberately set out to grow tobacco probably clawed a hole in the sandy loam of the Mayan peninsula, dropped in a handful of seed, covered the hole up again and waited for the seed to sprout. Since then, however, the whole business has become much more complicated.

70

Rapid expansion

It has also expanded rapidly. John Rolfe, for instance, the Jamestown colonist mentioned in the history chapter, took time off from wooing Princess Pocahontas to grow tobacco. In 1615 he exported 2,000 pounds of leaf to England from the Jamestown Colony. Less than 40 years later more than 1,400,000 pounds were shipped across the Atlantic from the New World.

Today tobacco is grown in 87 countries, including the United States, China, India and the Soviet Union. Cigar leaf, however, is pretty well confined to the United States, Indonesia, Brazil, the Philippines, Mexico, Colombia, Paraguay, Uruguay, Santo Domingo and Honduras.

With the exception of the United States areas (Connecticut, Massachusetts, Pennsylvania, Ohio, Florida, Georgia and Wisconsin), these countries lie almost entirely within 15 degrees of the equator and are generally associated with tropical climates. Soil requirements are less restrictive; tobacco of one kind or another (there are about 50 major varieties) will grow on anything—sandy loam to limestone-based hillside soil.

Crop rotation is practiced in a few areas—the planters in Sumatra and Java are very ambitious about this—but the bulk of the world's cigar leaf is produced with little or no attention to such niceties of agricultural technology. One tobacco crop can follow another year after year on the same plot without requiring cover crops or rotation.

There are several schools of thought on the degree of cultivation that should be done on tobacco land, but the concensus today is that a little (perhaps only some basic disk harrowing) goes a long way. The same is true of irrigation which, if overdone, can damage some cigar-leaf crops, and of fertilizer, which is generally used only sparingly.

Basically, then, growing tobacco for use in cigars is a pretty simple operation. The complexities stem from other factors. Great skill, experience, patience and expense are needed to produce the exact *quality* of leaf desired.

Three different types of tobacco go into every *good* cigar. A core of blended leaves known as "filler" is encased by a stouter, heavier leaf known as "binder." Both filler and binder are covered by the aristocrat of cigar leaf—the "wrapper."

71

Good filler tobacco must have a pleasant taste and burn freely and evenly. Binder tobacco is lighter, thinner and more elastic. Of course it must also taste good and have a pleasing aroma. Wrapper leaf is even thinner, with very fine veins. It must be of even color, open-grained, with a smooth, almost velvety texture. Its aroma, burning characteristics and taste are of prime importance.

The same plant can produce leaf that is suitable for each purpose, but today most crops are grown and later groomed for a specific use as filler, as binder or as wrapper. As might be expected, wrapper leaf is by far the most difficult to produce, and the costliest. It also, happily, brings the highest prices.

The world's finest

As stated earlier, some of the world's finest wrapper leaf now comes from fields in places such as Cameroon, Honduras and Nicaragua. In any discussion of wrapper the Housatonic Valley of Connecticut must also be mentioned. Connecticut has been one of America's traditional sources of uniformly excellent wrapper for decades. Connecticut tobaccos (called Connecticut Shade-Grown) are cultivated beneath vast cloth canopies which shield them from strong sunshine.

Note: Sumatra was once a synonym for quality in wrapper leaf. It no longer is. The island's tobacco industry was a casualty of World War II. The plantations deteriorated and collapsed during this conflict and, by American custom cigar standards, have never quite recovered.

The shade-grown variety of cigar wrapper was originally developed in Connecticut, and it is surprising to learn that Cuba now employs American shade-growing methods to improve her own product.

Filler leaf, grown under drier conditions and in fairly hot climates, is the basis for the flavor and aroma of the fine cigar. As indicated in a previous chapter, some of the most smokable filler imported into the United States today comes from Honduras, Mexico and Brazil. These countries grow an extraordinarily mild, aromatic tobacco.

72

The United States also supplies its own filler. Two states raise leaf with particularly distinctive character. Pennsylvania is one; the product is appropriately called Pennsylvania Seed Leaf. It grows mainly in Lancaster County. Ohio is the second state. Ohio Filler is raised primarily in the Miami Valley region.

In contrast to wrapper growing, which is usually quite an extensive operation, filler and binder tobacco are most often grown on small farms.

Ideally, cigar-filler leaf should be grown in rich, loose soil, but a reasonably good filler tobacco can be produced on virtually worn-out land. Rainfall is a prerequisite, but irrigation, oddly enough, can damage a filler crop, requiring extensive loosening of the soil.

Filler leaf is generally "topped" (a process that allows new buds to develop) lower than either binder or wrapper tobacco, with the top three or four leaves being removed along with the flower head. The stalks themselves are chopped off at ground level anywhere between two weeks and a month after topping. The stalks are allowed to wilt on the ground for several hours (preferably under a bright but not too hot sun) before they are spread on wooden laths for the curing process.

The best binder tobacco in the United States is grown in Connecticut, Pennsylvania, Massachusetts and Wisconsin, but several excellent varieties are also produced in the Caribbean (Jamaica) and Indonesia. The two best-known varieties are Connecticut Broadleaf and Connecticut Seed, both of which are "sun-grown," as opposed to "shade-grown."

Connecticut Broadleaf is an offshoot of a Maryland variety that was brought north in an effort to develop a wrapper-leaf industry. Connecticut seed was originally imported from the Caribbean although today it resembles none of the tobaccos found in that area. The binder tobacco of Wisconsin is grown from a seed called Spanish Comstock, which is also of West Indian origin.

The fields producing these binder types usually cover only four or five acres and, more often than not, are tilled by farmers who are growing other crops on adjacent tracts.

Fertilizer is kept to a minimum on most binder-leaf fields and irrigation is generally thought—at least in Connecticut—to cost more than it is worth.

73

Binder crops are not topped quite as low as filler leaf, although several of the top leaves are removed with the flower head. Binder leaf is stalk-cut in the same manner as filler, speared onto sticks in lots of five or six and left lying on the ground for a few hours to wilt. It is then taken to the curing barns.

Concerning American wrapper leaf:

The fine Connecticut Shade-Grown is raised in a 61-square-mile area on a narrow strip of land extending northward from Portland, Connecticut, through western Massachusetts to the border towns of Vermont and New Hampshire.

Imports—a key to quality

Currently tobacco imported from Brazil, Santo Domingo, Honduras, Nicaragua, Mexico and Cameroon is producing a high-quality cigar.

Shade-grown tobacco was tried out in Florida prior to its introduction in Connecticut in 1900, but production there and in Georgia has always been less than New England's. Georgia-Florida wrapper is considered to be of good quality. The Florida leaf, being extremely thin, does lend itself to the manufacture of the green "candela" wrappers now so popular in this country, and it is only in the South that they are produced.

The term candela refers to a particular heat-curing method which produces wrapper leaf of this distinctive color. Candela is the Spanish word for "flame" (see the following chapter on curing and aging).

Outside the United States, candela wrappers are also produced from the shade-grown tobacco crops in the West Indies. Tobacco plants that are grown there carry top leaves of suitable heaviness as well as an unusual elasticity and a pleasing sheen. The leaves at the top of wrapper-tobacco plants tend to be heavier than those at the bottom, and sometimes these top leaves show a reddish tint. In Connecticut, on the other hand, the top leaves have more of a tendency to turn green.

Wrapper crops are spaced more widely in the field than either filler or binder leaf, a practice that results in smaller leaves of light body and light weight per unit area.

Fertilizer (used in sparing qualtities) provides nitrogen and potassium to wrapper crops if the soil tends to be deficient in those elements, and the plants are cultivated frequently to keep the soil from packing around the bases of the plants.

Unlike other varieties, shade-grown wrapper leaf requires consistent irrigation since, sheltered by its canopy of cloth, natural rainfall is pretty well drained off. Good irrigation of wrapper leaf produces a thinner, lighter-colored leaf which ferments well and has a better burn.

Although wrapper leaf is now the premium tobacco crop in Connecticut, the first variety to be raised there was called "Shoestring." This tough and fibrous leaf was grown by the Indians long before the first colonists arrived. It wasn't until shortly before the Seven Years' War had ended in Europe, however, that cigar smoking gained any popularity in that state.

The colonel's legacy

Legend has it that the man responsible for this develop-

ment was Lieutenant Colonel Israel Putnam of Pomfret, Connecticut. Colonel Putnam, later a general in the Revolutionary
War, participated with the English in the siege of Havana as
part of the operations against Spanish territory. After the fall
of Havana, Putnam returned to Connecticut with three donkey
loads of booty—including a large store of the crude cigars then
popular among the Spanish of the West Indies.

Connecticut farmers began marketing their tobacco to the
cigar trade. It was popular as a wrapper and by 1825 was being
raised on a commercial scale. Then Maryland Broadleaf was
introduced in the 1830s.

But it lacked the fine texture, sweet taste and smooth
burning of Sumatra wrapper. Attempts were made to import
Sumatra Seed, but it did poorly. Although Connecticut crops
continued to supply the bulk of the filler and binder leaf,
American cigar manufacturers began relying more and more
upon Sumatra leaf for their wrappers.

Then came Connecticut Shade-Grown, which did for the
cigar industry what Henry Ford's Model T did for automobiles
—it turned a small industry into big business. This variety is the
end result of exhaustive experiments by the United States
Department of Agriculture's Division of Soils and the Connecticut Experiment Station at Windsor. According to the
Secretary of Agriculture at that time, "The leaf produced has
been so fine that the New York tobacco men say that it cannot
be told from the imported Sumatra leaf."

75

The key was shade. Sumatra seed, grown under what is
in effect a natural air-conditioning system utilizing the even
temperatures and cloudy skies of the tropics, produces exquisite
wrapper leaf.

Except for one small area near the Housatonic river at New
Milford, all Connecticut Shade-Grown is grown along the
Connecticut river, where the sandy loam is well protected by
surrounding hills.

Seeds for shade-grown wrapper leaf are treated gently,
being sown outdoors in glass-covered seed beds that have been
sterilized with live steam and chemicals to destroy any fungus
or weeds. Tobacco seeds, incidentally, are sometimes likened to
rabbits because of their reproductive capacities. Few other seeds

possess such enormous potential. On average, one tablespoon yields more than 1,500 pounds of leaf.

The seeds are grown and pampered in beds until the latter part of May; at this point they are transplanted to a more rugged environment in the fields. By this time the seedlings are six to eight weeks old, four to five inches high.

By this time, too, the fields have been plowed, harrowed and fertilized as necessary (or to suit the preference of the grower). The vital shade tents (usually of white or yellow cloth) are pitched on sturdy poles over the fields. Some farmers call them their "big tops," borrowing a circus term. Like so many numbers used in the tobacco industry, the material yardage of the big tops is enormous. It has been estimated that 50 million square yards of cloth are needed to provide New England tobacco with the proper shade each year.

The tents are held in place by 12-foot wooden poles that raise the cloth about eight feet above the ground. The poles are placed at 33-foot intervals and connected by heavy wire. The cloth, in 400-inch-wide strips, is spread across the wires and sewn in place. To produce just one acre of shade-grown tobacco requires 5,000 square yards of cloth, 55 12-foot cedar poles, 350 pounds of heavy galvanized wire and two tons of fertilizer.

Once the tobacco takes good root under the cloth it grows rapidly, developing a tall stalk and wide leaves. Control of insects and disease has developed rapidly in the last few years and, if proper care is shown, these are not considered much of a problem.

When the first buds appear, they are broken off to add strength to the stalk. The so-called sucker shoots at the bottom of the stalk, which tend to produce poor-quality leaf, are removed just prior to harvesting, usually early in July.

The leaves are carefully picked (or "primed") when they reach maturity. Bottom leaves ripen more slowly and are the last to be picked.

Picked leaves need delicate care, being kept absolutely flat and shaded from the sun in the curing shed, where they are hung high to avoid curing in piles. Leaves are sewn in pairs back to back, by a needle and thread through the stem of each

leaf. Then 20 to 22 pairs of them are sewn onto a lath, sometimes called a "stick," which is suspended from overhead cross-
bars in the curing shed.

A complicated process

The growing of the tobacco is, of course, only the beginning. It still must be cured, fermented, sorted and graded.

Ironically, it is in this beginning—the growing—that one of
the major cigar industry crises is shaping up today. With the
demand for cigars soaring in the United States, cigar makers
are scrambling for the world supplies of quality leaf at low
prices.

There is tobacco which is the peer of or better than West
Indian leaf grown in the United States and other countries.
Everyone wants quality, however. The world supply is subject to highly competitive buying. To maintain their traditional
quality, United States custom-grade cigar makers must compete.

"Filler is becoming the big problem," states one former
manufacturer of high-quality cigars. "Good filler is in short
supply. Makers who want to sustain a high-quality level are
going to have to get out into the fields and become almost as
knowledgeable as growers are. They're going to have to start
following crop and weather reports. They're going to have to
start going right out to the farmers, at home and abroad, and
buying directly from them. . . . Many makers today buy on
the basis of the samples sent them, and that's not going to work
too well much longer. They're sometimes not getting the quality
they think they're paying for. . . . Go to the farmers. This is
the way to do it. I always did it myself when I was in business.
. . . You buy as much as you can afford when crops are good
and keep it in reserve against years when they're inferior. . . .
Anybody in this country today who's producing 100 million
cigars or more, and who wants to maintain quality, is going to
have to buy in everybody's backyard."

77

8

A touch of seasoning

Old age is the cure

As is true of many complicated subjects, the process of curing cigar tobacco can also be described in simplistic terms.

Curing, or seasoning, is the means by which the sap is removed from tobacco. Flues, fires or the heat from the sun may be employed, depending on whether the tobacco is to be used for cigars, pipes, cigarettes or plug.

This definition of course has the shortcoming of all simplistic definitions. It does not begin to describe the time and effort required in preparing tobacco for any use, cigar use in particular. It does not begin to tell the many things which can go wrong during the process. Nor does it begin to set the penalties on carelessness and failure.

As might be expected with a plant so sensitive that its growing conditions must be precisely regulated, the curing of tobacco is a difficult and delicate process depending as much upon subjective evaluation as upon mechanical regulation. Exactly the right temperature and humidity must be maintained at all times to produce the quality tobacco demanded by cigar smokers.

The actual process varies according to geography, ranging

from those countries that depend entirely on nature to those that employ complicated artificial drying methods. The bulk of Brazilian Bahia tobacco, for instance, is cured in the open air or, at best, in open-ended sheds or lean-tos. In Sumatra charcoal fires heat the curing sheds; in the United States, gas and oil heaters are utilized.

Fine cigar leaf is air-cured much in the same manner that the finer cigarette tobaccos such as Burley and Maryland are processed. Basically, air curing involves three stages: 1. wilting; 2. browning; 3. drying.

The key to seasoning and curing is proper ventilation inside the curing shed. The importance of this cannot be stressed too heavily. Humidity must be maintained at a specific ratio to the temperature, and to do so seasoning men follow the "Rule of Ten." This rule states that the humidity percentage and the Fahrenheit temperature are to be held ten digits apart during seasoning and curing. For example, when the humidity is 60, the temperature should be 70 degrees F.

If humidity is allowed to reach too high a level, mold, rot or "pole sweat" may set in. Pole sweat is a form of deterioration known to occur only in tobacco plants.

The inside temperature, in turn, is maintained at a level five to ten degrees above that of the outside air. It is not allowed to go above 100 degrees F. if possible.

Ventilation control varies:

There are favorite methods peculiar to each tobacco region. In Connecticut wooden sheds are built with a single ridge roof than can be levered open to allow air to flow in and out without exposing the drying leaf to rain. The sides of these sheds are constructed of a series of movable slats resembling Venetian blinds. They can be opened or shut mechanically to control humidity.

Connecticut sheds are subdivided into 16-foot-square sections called "bents." By Connecticut arithmetic, four bents are the required space for curing a single acre of wrapper leaf.

In Florida the curing sheds are larger than Connecticut sheds and their side ventilators are set vertically rather than laterally. Florida *barns,* as they are called (not curing sheds), will hold approximately 17,500 sticks of tobacco leaf.

A regional practice

There are other regional practices. In Florida and Connecticut the sheds are used solely for processing tobacco. Pennsylvania and Wisconsin growers, however, often store other seasonal crops in them or use them to house farm animals.

In Sumatra curing sheds are primitive structures compared to those in the United States. They resemble old American Indian council houses, having long sloping roofs bolstered by heavily gabled ends. These roofs slope almost to the ground and the sides are thatched with palm fronds. As in Connecticut, parts of the roof are hinged to allow proper ventilation. (Note: Sumatra still produces some of the world's finest wrapper leaf.)

One reason Connecticut Shade-Grown is lighter in color than Sumatra wrapper is that the firing is primarily part of the basic curing process. In Indonesia, on the other hand, the smoldering charcoal is used only for aiding the circulation of air when the weather is so humid that the tobacco is in danger of spoiling.

Air circulation is also a problem in the United States when the fresh leaf is first hung in the curing shed. The leaves are so full of sap and are hung so close together that one touches the one next to it, blocking the necessary flow of air.

Within a week, however, wilting shrinks the still-vibrant leaves enough so there is sufficient room between them to allow proper ventilation.

The wilting process requires only from two to four days. Once the tip of the leaf begins turning brown, wilting is regarded as completed and the actual curing process (browning) begins.

In the beginning, the tobacco is heated from two to three hours each day—or sometimes only once a day if weather conditions are sufficiently damp. The leaf quickly turns brown all over. Daily firings are then maintained to dry it out evenly. Planters never fire at night, to allow moisture in the stem and the flat wide part of the leaf (lamina) to spread to the leaf extremities, thus producing an evenness of tone and color.

During the process of drying out the stem, the ventilators are shut each night unless the weather has been particularly hot and dry. As already stated, the entire idea of curing tobacco is to remove all the natural sap from the leaf, but this must be done slowly to retain the proper coloring and texture. The whole process usually takes from three to five weeks. Oddly, those leaves which are the last picked—or last primed, as tobacco farmers say—require the longest curing time.

Fast-curing candelas

The green candela wrappers produced in the South (and so popular in the United States today) require only three to four days of curing before they are completely dried out. Stalk-cut tobacco, whether for filler or binder purposes, is cured in the same manner as prime wrapper leaf but perhaps with a bit less tender loving care.

Once the curing process has been completed, the leaves are taken down, unthreaded from their sticks and tied into bundles preparatory to fermentation. This is often done at night or following a night in which the ventilators have been left open. The reason is that by this time the tobacco leaf is too dry to handle without restoring just a bit of moisture to keep it from crumbling. When leaves are in the proper condition for handling, they are said to be "in case."

Stalk-cut tobacco leaf is stripped from the stalks before being bundled, a process that takes several days. With wrapper leaf, which has been primed leaf by leaf, there is no such problem.

It is important to segregate leaves picked from different positions on the plant stalk and to further segregate leaves from different primings, or pickings. These leaves ferment at different rates of speed and must be timed to finish fermenting together.

The fermentation of tobacco resembles the fermentation of wine and of bread dough. It is simply a chemical change brought about in vegetable substances by any one of several means.

In wine making, fermentation is induced to produce alcohol. In tobacco fermentation, the gradual chemical changes are induced by certain handling and storing techniques to convert

81

sap and plant cell matter into essences and oils that give cigar tobaccos their flavors and aromas.

Fermentation is said by some experts to be the most vital step in cigar-tobacco preparation. Perhaps it is, perhaps it isn't; tobacco men will argue the matter endlessly. Unfermented (or carelessly fermented) leaf often burns unevenly. It can show a "rose petal effect"; that is, the leaf at the burning end separates into sections resembling rose petals. Such sloppily handled tobacco also lacks aroma and is acrid to the taste. Well-fermented tobacco possesses delicate color, fine texture and good burning characteristics.

Not all unfermented tobacco should be condemned out of hand. Brazilian tobacco is seldom fermented, or only lightly, and yet Brazil produces some of the world's finest cigars. Consider Florida candela wrapper also. Candela is never fermented and only lightly cured so that its characteristic green shade will be kept intact.

Skipping fermentation, then, can be said to be as vital a step as fermentation itself. Whether tobacco is fermented or not, it is the planter's processing skill which determines its quality in the end.

If fermented, cigar leaf is usually treated in the warehouse to which it is taken after leaving the curing sheds. The tobacco arrives at the warehouse in man-high cases. Wooden hogsheads were once used as containers; as a matter of fact, the cases are still called hogsheads although they may no longer be of true barrel shape or made of wood.

82

5,000 pounds of leaf

Tobacco fermentation is started by dumping the bundles of leaf from their cases into piles called "bulks" on platforms. Each bulk weighs from 3,000 to 5,000 pounds. Actual fermentation begins when the heat of oxidation builds up inside each bulk; heat cannot escape easily because there is no ventilation deep inside the bulk. In tobacco parlance such tobacco is said to be "in bulk." The heat buildup beginning the fermentation is called "sweating."

A long thermometer is jabbed into the center of every bulk

to record its heat level. As the temperature climbs, the bulks are rearranged, center leaves being moved to the outside of the pile, outside leaves to the center. This is done every eight to ten days. The purpose of the process is to sweat the leaves uniformly. It is at the center of the bulk, of course, that fermentation heat is the highest. This "turning" process (i.e., building new bulks out of old ones) goes on for as long as two months until the fermentation reaches the point where it will result in the most delicate taste, finest burning quality and smoothest, most elastic texture.

This process is pretty standard, but again there are variations in some details, depending on geographical location. In Sumatra, for example, center-bulk temperatures are allowed to go as high as 140 degrees F. In Florida the bulks are turned as soon as the center temperature reaches about 115 degrees. In the West Indies, where the bulks are much smaller, the center-bulk heat will rarely exceed 110 degrees.

In the past few years, cigar manufacturers have speeded up the whole operation by loosely packing the leaf in cardboard cartons and covering the cartons with plastic sheets. The cartoned tobacco is then maintained at a consistent high temperature. This new method allows for much more precise control of the entire process and results, as might be expected, in a much more controlled level of quality.

Stalk-cut tobaccos destined for binder or filler use are received in fairly dry condition at the warehouse. (Stalk-cut tobaccos are harvested by cutting down the entire plant and then removing the leaves.) They are subsquently conditioned by forcing steam through the bundles.

Once thoroughly steamed, the leaves are tipped, threshed (this applies to short filler only) and piled in large bulks. Center-bulk temperatures for fermenting binder and filler tobaccos are generally kept around the 110-degree mark. American filler tobacco, incidentally, is regarded as one of the world's mildest because of its carefully controlled fermentation.

A matter of happenstance

Other countries rarely devote as much attention to fermen-

83

tation as the United States does. This is evidenced by the uneven quality of much of the cigar leaf produced elsewhere. In the West Indies only mild fermentation is allowed, and in Brazil the process is virtually happenstance, as already indicated. Brazilian tobacco is fermented only while it lies in the warehouse waiting for grading. Yet, Brazil produces some excellent cigars.

With filler and binder tobaccos, it is possible for the cigar manufacturer himself to restart fermentation if he thinks it necessary following a period of dry storage. Once the initial process has been halted with the more delicate wrapper leaf, however, it cannot be restarted.

After fermentation has been completed, the leaves are carefully examined for quality, color, texture and moisture. Usually they are then sorted into about 20 different grades. All colors will not be present in every crop, but about 14 different shades can be recognized from a single field. The leaves, usually about 15 to 20 from each plant, vary in size from 8½ to 18 inches. Once they have been graded, they are sorted according to size, packed in wooden cases and stored for another six weeks of final fermentation.

84

More than half of the grading and sizing of American tobacco crops is done in Puerto Rico, a practice that was born of manpower needs in the United States during World War II. The leaves are shipped in large lots. Some of these wrappers sized and graded in Puerto Rico are utilized in that island's extensive cigar-manufacturing industry, but most of them are returned to the United States.

The actual grading shed can be any well-lit building in which the tobacco can be kept at fairly constant levels of humidity and temperature. Generally the thinnest and finest leaves of the plant are given the highest gradings.

A quality leaf from a good crop is so thin and delicate as to be virtually transparent. Poor-quality leaves are heavier and have little elasticity. Except in Florida, where the color green is preferred for candela wrapper leaf, the best color is a lustrous light tan. Mottled or mixed colors are less desirable and bring much lower prices on the market.

When the leaf has been graded, it is tied with raffia into

Burley tobacco awaiting the auctioneer in Frankfort, Kentucky.

fan-shaped "hands" containing about 40 leaves each. The hands are laid flat on the wooden platforms again, then pressed firmly into baling boxes. Each leaf layer is protected from the next by soft paper. About 150 pounds of tobacco are pressed into each bale. The bales themselves are then covered with grass mats woven in Borneo or with a newer paper matting produced in the United States. Both types of wrapping allow the baled tobacco to continue to "breathe."

The moisture content of the bales is carefully measured to allow for pressurized packing that will not damage the leaf. It is considered of particular importance that the midrib of the leaf be unbroken. Once baled, the tobacco now ages in the same manner that flue-cured tobaccos (which are not fermented) are aged.

Grading processes are fairly similar throughout the cigar-leaf-growing world. In the Caribbean, however, the light better-quality leaf known as "Regazo" tends to a more reddish brown. In Sumatra the most desirable color of the Deli wrapper is more of a gray-brown with a slight hint of olive green.

A precisely graded crop

Sumatran grading, incidentally, was for years considered

the world's most precise because the entire crop was produced for the world market: it was sold at auction in Amsterdam and Bremen in lots that had to be absolutely uniform and consistent in quality. Most other countries, including the United States, grow crops mainly for specific, precontracted manufacturers. Thus, such precise grading is not required.

The grading of binder tobacco is much less sophisticated than that of wrapper leaf. The chief concerns for natural binders are texture and size. Color (since the binder tobacco is used only in the inside of cigars) hardly enters into it. The most important consideration is size, because uniformity in length and thickness forestalls waste in the cutting process.

Filler tobacco is judged and purchased more by the geographical area from which it comes rather than by any breakdown of grading values. The subsequent sorting is done by the purchaser according to the manufacturer's needs.

Puerto Rican tobacco is sorted according to a 20-grade classification set up by the United States Department of Agriculture, but basically there are six main categories of filler tobacco, each carrying a standard price.

In countries such as Brazil, where the cigar's filler, binder and wrapper all come from the same plant (but from different heights on the stem), the grading is much more elementary. Leaf is simply sorted for use as filler, binder and wrapper. The upper leaves of the plant, incidentally, are heavier and more aromatic.

Leaf strength is important in the grading of filler tobacco only when the manufacturer is producing large cigars or in cases where the cigars are still being hand rolled in traditional fashion. In both cases long unbroken pieces of lamina called "blankets" are needed and will carry a higher rating when graded. And upon that rating, of course, depends the price.

It takes more than a year from the time the first seed beds are planted until the leaf reaches the manufacturer. A year— this is a long time if one thinks in other terms—jail sentences, for instance. In terms of tobacco, however, it has a different meaning.

To the maker of fine cigars, a year may be considered only the beginning.

86

9

"First take a little filler..."

How they're made—
82-12-6 is the magic combination

One of the most unlikable women ever to smoke a cigar was the late Ma Barker, who took her sons robbing and killing with Thompson submachine guns in the Midwest during the 1930s. It is said that this unusual matriarch once boxed one of her boys' ears for suggesting that the clan drive to Florida and rob some of the big cigar-factory payrolls there.

"Not while I still love a good cigar, stupid. It's bad luck to do harm to the things you love," she is supposed to have said, scolding the boy. Then she added with a sigh, "But I sure wouldn't mind going through one sometimes just to see how they're made."

Mother Barker never entered a cigar factory in her life, but if she had, she might have been surprised.

The manufacture of cigars is basically quite simple.

In the first step, a quantity of filler tobacco is formed into the size and shape of the cigar desired.

Next, this wad of filler is bound together with a layer of binder tobacco, which can be either real leaf or synthetic homogenized tobacco leaf (described later in this chapter).

Third, filler wad and binder tobacco are covered with

wrapper. In a fine cigar this wrapper is always of natural leaf.

With variations and substitutions, that is all there is to the process—a three-step combination of filler, binder and wrapper.

A typical cigar may contain 82 percent filler, 12 percent binder and 6 percent wrapper. These proportions will vary according to the size, shape, brand and quality of a given cigar. Paradoxically, an inexpensive cigar may contain disproportionate amounts of expensive filler. The explanation is that portions of wrapper leaf trimmed from cigars are sometimes fed back into the filler blend so that the actual wrapper-leaf content may be as high as 20 percent.

Traditionally, cigars have been hand rolled. Hand rolling is a practice that once provided hundreds of thousands of workers with steady employment but outrageously low wages and substandard working conditions. Today the wages are higher and the working conditions improved, but steady employment as a cigar roller is difficult to come by. There just are not that many cigars being hand rolled anymore.

88

One unusual aspect of the cigar-making industry in the pre-automation age led to the rise of labor leader Samuel Gompers and, eventually, to the founding of the American Federation of Labor. Gompers was a "shop reader" in a New York cigar factory. Shop reader was a unique position first established in the Caribbean by the local cigar makers who found that their trade, while demanding considerable manual dexterity, required very little mental concentration. To occupy their thoughts, the workers would hire someone to read to them, and the workers themselves paid the reader's wages.

Gompers came off the streets of New York City to take a job as a cigar roller in a factory manned primarily by German immigrants. Because he spoke and read both German and English fluently, and because he had a fine speaking voice, he was picked by his fellow workers to be a reader. Allowed to select his own subject matter, the astute Gompers invariably read from books dealing with labor theory and socialism.

"Valley of the Dolls"

With the advent of modern machinery, the reader has

disappeared today from American factories, but in Brazil and the West Indian the practice still exists. And reports from the Caribbean indicate that labor problems and socialism are still popular subjects with the factory readers. It is a little different in Brazil, however, where a reader is as likely to choose "The Valley of the Dolls" or "Naked Came a Stranger" as he is "The Economic Basis of the Brazilian Labor Movement from 1938 to 1945." The former choices apparently have a sharply curtailing effect on absenteeism. Nobody presumably wants to miss the next chapter.

The advent of machine-made cigars in the late 1920s virtually drove the factory readers from the American scene. It was the American Tobacco Company that first began manufacturing cigars mechanically. Called "Cremo" cigars, they were advertised rather unsubtly in big, bold type: "Why run the risk of cigars made by dirty yellowed fingers?"

The idea was to shock the smoking public into buying machine-made cigars, but all it did was shock. Cigar sales in the United States nosedived from 8.5 billion cigars in 1920 to only 5.5 billion in 1939. It has only been in the last few years that cigar sales have again reached the 8-billion mark.

Of all cigars sold today, fewer than 5 percent are hand rolled. The rest comes off an assembly line of machines that can turn out cigars at a rate of about 650 an hour. By contrast, the most highly skilled hand rollers in the world can only hope to produce, at most, about 200 a day.

Whether cigars are machine-made or hand rolled, the first step in the manufacturing process is the same. The leaves must be "stemmed" (the midrib removed), and this can only be done after the leaf has been resoftened by moistening, as redundant as that might seem after all the drying out it has gone through. Once the leaves have been stemmed, the various tobaccos (wrapper, binder and filler) must be fed to either the workman or the machine in just the proper blend.

In early times when cigars were exclusively hand rolled, filler leaf was usually delivered to the manufacturer in what was called "long" form, pieces as large as the full length of the cigar. This was convenient for hand rollers but not for machines. Today "short" filler is used as well. Short filler is just

89

what the name says it is, small pieces and lengths of filler that are shorter than the full length of the cigar. Long filler is the best. There are, however, certain advantages for using short filler: the manufacturer can use more of the crop he purchases. Pieces too short for use in long-filler cigars are long enough for short-filler cigars. Also, the manufacturer can blend several different types of short filler to change the properties of his cigars.

After the filler has been "formed," the binder leaf is added to make what is called a "bunch." The bunches are then molded into shape. (The molded bunches are often subjected to a bit more heat to dry them out again.) Next comes the wrapping.

A matter of care

With wrapper leaf so costly, extreme care is taken to cut it precisely without undue waste. Once cut to the exact size of the cigar, the wrapper is wound onto the bunch in a tight spiral, beginning at the fire end of the cigar and progressing to the head end. If wrapped in the other direction, it will unwind as the cigar is smoked, an experience more than one neophyte smoker has undergone after lighting the wrong end of his cigar.

Usually the upper surface of the leaf becomes the outside surface of the cigar. If a lighter candela shade is desired, however, and if the veins are fine enough, then the leaf is wrapped with the underside uppermost. To accommodate both processes, factories must have both left-hand and right-hand spiraling machines so that cigars may be rolled with either side out.

Some cigar makers still see to it that all the cigars for one box are left-handed or right-handed, so that each box presents a uniform appearance. Once in the box, many cigars are then gently pressed to give them a smooth finish.

Competition has spawned the great cigar variety we know today. Each factory tries to produce brands with unique characteristics that belong to them alone. With this in mind most of them buy tobacco from the same farms, year after year, in order to maintain an even quality.

The advantages of hand rolling are mainly those of individual care and inspection. In fact, in many hand-rolling fac-

90

tories mechanical aids are used. Evident in almost all such plants are the molds that form bunches before wrapping, and "aprons" that roll the binder around the bunch.

There are eight primary moves in hand rolling a cigar:

1. The hand operator gathers a handful of filler leaf (which comprises the main body of the cigars). With skillful pressing and prodding he compresses the filler into an even, well-shaped bulk.

2. Onto this bulk (or body) he rolls a single leaf of binder tobacco to form a bunch.

3. The bunch is trimmed to the required size and any too-long filler leaves are cut off.

4. The bunch is then laid aside momentarily. The operator now trims the delicate wrapper leaf to the precise shape and size needed.

5. With quick, deft movements the operator encases the bunch in the wrapper and rolls this outer leaf on with a spiral motion.

6. Next the small flap (called a "flag") at the end is sealed over the head of the cigar to hold the wrapper in place.

7. A touch of harmless, tasteless, colorless adhesive (usually gum tragacanth) is applied to the flag to hold it in place.

8. Finally, a flat block is used to roll the cigar back and forth on a board and give it uniform, cylindrical shape.

Once cigars have been rolled, they are turned over to a "selector." This individual, hired for his uncompromising, fussy nature, grades cigars for boxing according to color. During the past 60 years, light-colored (claro) cigars have gained great popularity. Smokers have come to believe that the lighter the shade, the milder the smoke. This is erroneous. Erroneous or not, however, the belief did affect cigar marketing. However, this trend has been changing rapidly in recent years.

Time to mature

Even though manufacture is complete at this point, cigars are still not ready to be put to the match and enjoyed. They must be "put to sleep" in storage (at least 90 days is the recommended time) to mature. The lighter and milder varieties mature quickly once they are stored. Fuller-bodied cigar tobacco needs longer rest.

The maturing process is much like the earlier fermentation and is basically a matter of time, temperature and humidity.

How is maturation determined? By moisture content primarily.

When properly matured, most cigars will retain moisture content of 11 or 12 percent. Higher humidity results in sogginess. Soggy cigars will not remain lighted. Less humidity leaves cigars crusty and brittle. Some dark cigars require nine months or longer to mature.

Storage care is still needed after maturation is complete. Ideally a manufacturer will keep his cigars awhile longer in chambers in which humidity is maintained at about 60 to 67 percent and temperatures between the mid-60s and mid-70s. Under ideal conditions, cigars which are still too wet or dry for distribution to market will "settle down" to peak smoking level in one or two months. This humidity and temperature control is critical. Rapid swings in either direction can do great damage —wrapper separation, for example.

To some degree, the aging process improves most varieties of cigars. Sumatras are regarded as being at their best when they are between three and four years old. They can be smoked with pleasure with each succeeding year. Connecticut tobacco, less strong matures more quickly but tends to fade more quickly also.

The major innovation in the manufacture of cigars in the last 20 years has been the development of reconstituted tobacco sheet, a process that utilizes the entire tobacco plant (leaves, stems, ribs) and results in a wide, flat sheet of tobacco that is readily adapted to machines. It is used in cigars primarily as binder.

The reconstituted sheet is used by virtually all manufacturers of inexpensive cigars. Its main value lies in the fact that it is the only way in which damaged leaves and leftovers in the field can be turned into a reasonably mild and inexpensive tobacco.

A great deal of any binder crop (up to 40 percent in some areas) ordinarily goes to waste. When turned into reconstituted sheet, a given field of tobacco will cover more than twice as many cigars as will natural leaf binder, according to a recent report from the United States Department of Agriculture.

A soupy mixture

Briefly, to manufacture tobacco sheet, tobacco ground to fine dust is mixed with water or some inorganic solvent to form a soupy mixture called slurry (a paper-manufacturing term). Adhesives and any other additives (such as flavoring) are then included and the mixture is poured to spread flat so that it will dry and form sheets. The final product is then rolled tightly on bobbins and can be unrolled and cut to exact sizes desired by manufacturers. The process is similar to the paper-manufacturing process. The sheet resembles paper. Indeed, it can be called paper made from tobacco pulp instead of wood pulp.

The development of sheet for cigars is generally credited to a German scientist and was first used in 1935. It has proven particularly valuable in small-cigar manufacture.

Small cigars, like cigarettes, are produced on the continuous rod principle, a process first patented in 1880. The sheet is wound from the aforementioned bobbins. At the same time a regulated amount of tobacco scrap is poured continuously onto the sheet. It is then rolled and gummed mechanically and finally sliced up into desired lengths.

For the manufacturer (particularly the little-cigar manufacturer), sheet tobacco is a lifesaver in terms of economy. By varying the amounts of various additives that go into the sheet, the manufacturer can obtain precisely the flavor, aroma and combustion qualities he desires in his cigars.

For the cigar connoisseur, however, there is no substitute for the real thing. Homogenized leaf, additives or flavorings can never replace fine cigar tobaccos. Even Ma Barker, on receiving such doctored cigars, might have felt she was being held up.

93

10

Turning over
a new leaf

Still needed: a good, inexpensive cigar

"There are plenty of good five-cent cigars. . . . The trouble is, they all cost fifteen cents."

This was the late cowboy humorist Will Rogers talking. The time was the American Depression, and his topic was inflationary costs. As usual, Rogers was having sly, satirical fun. His statement was close to the truth then; it is still applicable today.

Cigar costs are up. Quality in many cases is down. There are still nickel cigars, true enough. But now as then the likelihood of a *good* nickel cigar made of natural tobacco filler, binder and wrapper is remote. (We are not speaking here of small cigars, many of which cost five cents or less, and many of which are quite good.)

There are fine cigars available, however, and if a smoker shops carefully, he (or she) need not pay high for the low quality Will Rogers spoke of. There are quality cigars to be found at reasonable prices . . . if a smoker takes the trouble to find them. The prices might surprise even Will Rogers. Some cost only about 15 cents.

This book began with a chapter referring to something

called the custom-quality cigar. The succeeding pages spoke of cigars good and bad. It is fitting that the book should end with more information on the quality cigar, the American-made product in particular.

What is the status of such cigars today? Where are they (and all cigars) going tomorrow? What can both the beginning smoker and the connoisseur expect for whatever price they pay? The truth is that the American cigar smoker is price-oriented.

In the economy cigar field (say, 30 cents and under) United States manufacturers have always worried about holding prices down than about raising quality. They try to do both, of course, but holding the price line comes first. There is a reason: among United States cigar smokers there is fierce loyalty to price and almost no loyalty to brand.

According to one diversified retailer who deals only in custom cigars, "A cigarette man stays with one brand over long periods, no matter how much it moves up in price. Cigarette prices are pretty much standard for most brands anyway and an increase doesn't seem to matter much to him.

"It does, however, to a cigar man. A cigar man is what I'd call a price-range addict. He has fixed in his mind a certain price he'll pay and he won't pay more if he can help it, no matter what he has to smoke. He switches around a great deal anyway, always looking for the perfect cigar for his price. And if the cigar he's been smoking goes up, he'll try another in the old price range. Maybe he won't even miss the kind he's been smoking before."

95

A bit of digression

Some digression is in order here.

Custom buying habits are not the only cigar-industry problem. A complex marketing and retailing structure is another. One particular problem is the tax structure.

The United States Internal Revenue Service taxes cigars by price. All cigars fall into one of seven IRS-prescribed tax classes. Class A (cigars retailing for no more than 2½ cents apiece) enjoys the lowest tax rate. Class G (cigars selling for 20 cents apiece and up) is taxed heaviest.

With this in mind, the manufacturer's obsession with price is understandable. The thing he dislikes most is seeing one of his cigar brands become so costly to produce that he must raise the retail price, high enough to lift it another IRS tax notch.

Another problem: the cigarette companies that are now invading the cigar field. The friendly but remote rivalry that once prevailed between cigar and cigarette producers has turned into the fierce infighting so common among competing soap companies.

The cause is simple. Cigarette sales have been dropping since the 1964 publication by the United States government of *Smoking and Health: Report of the Advisory Committee to the Surgeon General of the Public Health Service*. American cigarette sales are down from nearly 530 billion per year in 1967 to an estimated 500 billion in 1970. (At the time this was written, the final figures for 1970 were not available.) To fill the void left by these losses, cigarette manufacturers want a part of the cigar market.

Still another problem: retail cigar-market expansion born of the struggle to stay in the black. Cigar manufacturers must seek customers from population groups wooed only halfheartedly until now. One is the so-called "New Generation," made up of men and women from 21 through 35. The senior vice president of one of the oldest American cigar houses stated in the June 20, 1970 issue of *Business Week*: "Our youth market used to start at about age 47; now we have an opportunity to attract younger men—and at a time when many cigarette smokers are searching for substitutes."

The above facts are offered only as a sampling of cigar industry affairs; they represent only the top of the iceberg, so to speak.

This book is concerned with the pleasure, not the business of cigars, however. A discussion in depth of the commercial complexities has only a limited place here. The individual with serious research interest in these areas should seek information at such places as the United States Department of Agriculture and the United States Department of Commerce, both in Washington, D.C.; the public libraries; the cigar companies themselves; the Cigar Institute of America. All are cooperative and welcome queries. Still, of all the devils besetting the cigar industry, none is more nettlesome than the customer obsession with price. This has directly influenced and changed cigar quality (often for the worse) more than any one other factor.

Production shortcuts

For more years than they like to remember, cigar makers with a conscience and a feeling for quality have been relying, however reluctantly, more and more upon production shortcuts and economies—and the cigar tobacco technology has supplied them as needed. Homogenized tobacco leaf is but one economy-spawned development. Manufacturers justify its use by claiming that consistently fine cigars can be made today by using the paperlike sheet as wrapper. This is certainly a hedge, a substitute for the real thing. Deep in his heart there is not a maker anywhere who is not also a cigar connoisseur himself and who would not prefer to wrap his cigars in real leaf with traditional methods—and the expense be damned.

Much about cigars today reflects the price squeeze and the pressure to open new retail markets:

■ The subtle advertising aligning cigars with the "good life" and the young, active, successful, adventurous people supposedly populating this land.

■ The proliferation of the slim and short cigars. They bear names bringing the compactness and sleekness of bullets to mind. They require less tobacco and work and are therefore cheaper to manufacture than are "big" cigars. These slims, small cigarillos, whatever they are called, are today the largest-selling cigars in the country.

Of nearly eight billion cigars of all varieties sold in 1969, these midgets numbered nearly three-quarters of a billion, or approximately one-tenth of the total.

Cigar purists loathe them, especially the ones with flavorings and plastic tips. They are scorned as candy cigars, toys and baby pacifiers. Indeed, many small cigars currently manufactured would not appeal to even the most permissive cigar connoisseur; they are scrap-filled and the flavorings only serve to cover harsh tobacco qualities.

97

The plastic tips are a necessary safety device; they hold the smoking ends together. Many small cigars are sheet-wrapped and therefore fragile, breaking under handling or even lip pressure. Without plastic tips they tend to spill tobacco onto the smokers' tongues.

There *are* fine quality mini-cigars, of course. For short-time smoking (after lunch, before returning to work, for example) there are no finer smokes than the quality American, Danish and Dutch whiffs found in quality tobacconists' shops.

The terms "small" and "little" as applied here embrace all mini-cigars, from the very popular tipped variety on down the scale in size. Some industry spokesmen, however, claim the words specifically refer to the pencil-thin three-inchers open at both ends, and to no others.

Other new approaches to the marketing problem:

■ Introduction of the aforementioned flavorings. Today a smoker can buy cigars (generally small ones) which taste of menthol, cherry, rum, honey, coffee.

■ Introduction of novelty aroma-producing substances. These take little away from the natural tobacco taste but give off pleasant scents. Chocolate is one. "It smelled as though someone had opened a box of French candy in the room," said a girl who smoked one recently.

■ Experimentation with colored plastic tips. These have not caught on with the buyer so far, incidentally.

■ The appeal to women to smoke small cigars both for stylishness and a switch to some tobacco form considered less risky than cigarettes. ("Would you offer a lady a cigar?") The Cigar Institute of America estimates that ". . . some 200,000 American women are now smoking cigars in public." The CIA further estimates three times this number are "closet smokers." They puff their cigars in privacy and will not come out until they have perfected graceful cigar handling form so they can avoid being jeered at or criticized.

Two generalizations

Two generalizations come up again and again in any evaluation of cigar quality today.

One, the big producers are not turning out inexpensive (below 30 cents) quality cigars that can be held up as custom grade.

Two, the smaller manufacturers are the last strongholds of quality—because of their handcrafting—though they, too, must technically be considered mass producers since their output is in the millions per year.

Both statements are flawed, too broad, too simplistic. There are fine national brand-production cigars, some selling below the critical price. There are terrible "small label" cigars. One New York man who has spent his career as a cigar maker by trudging through tobacco fields in various countries states today:

"Ah, the romance of the custom-made cigar! Some manufacturers still sustain a few custom operations just so they can put the label on the box and jack up the price. 'Handmade' can be a joke on the customer. There's nothing wrong with machine cigars. If made properly, I'll smoke a machine cigar any day."

This retired manufacturer raises a point concerning the use of the word "custom." He feels there are few examples of true custom cigars made today. Few manufacturers can afford to make them. Few smokers can afford to smoke them. They are almost exclusively the cigars of the wealthy.

99

He applies an earlier strict dictionary meaning to the word: "Made or done to order; as, custom clothes. Manufacturing, or dealing in, things made to order; as, custom clothes" (*Webster's New Collegiate Dictionary*, G. and C. Merriam, Springfield, Massachusetts, 1956). To him, the word applies to a cigar especially produced by a maker to one individual's taste and specification and produced for no other. (The previously mentioned "he-man special" made for actor John Wayne is one example.)

The manufacturer says, "For example, most people think the term 'custom rolled in Tampa' still means hand rolled. Custom rolled in Tampa is rot. Most Tampa cigars are rolled by machine."

He gives ground, however, and concedes the word "custom" has also come to stand for "quality" in certain cigars today. "I'll buy the word if it isn't slaughtered the way it is so often when applied to so many products," he says. "I'll buy it if it truly means high quality in a cigar."

Any cigar that is truly custom quality will probably still involve some manual operations somewhere in its manufacture. The men who make and sell these cigars, as do the men who produce and sell vintage wines, feel that the touch of the human hand still makes a difference.

Custom means quality, then. Quality means custom. Smokers must accept this overlapping meaning. This does not mean they must compromise. True custom cigars may be beyond reach of all but a few, but quality cigars are not.

At what price does the smoker cross the custom-quality threshold? This is a difficult question to answer in general terms.

In some shops 15 cents buys a custom-quality cigar. Thirty cents buys the best. Prices are even lower by the box.

In other shops 30 cents is only the beginning.

One answer is that so much depends upon the tobacconist himself. The custom quality is there at a good price. He must only know how to find it.

Is he a cigar lover himself? Does he really know brands and how they are made? (There are differences. The 20-cent cigar from one house is not always the same as the 20-center from a competing house.) Does he buy up wholesale lots he can sell under his own label as "house brands"? (These are often excellent and low in price.) Does he perhaps own or hold interest in a small factory? (Some dealers do. This represents a plus for the smoker. A dealer-owner can exercise firm quality control.)

The tobacconist himself determines to a great degree the value the smoker receives for whatever price he pays. Where price seriously enters into cigar purchases, it is said that the tobacconist's expertise is the smoker's biggest discount.

The future for cigars

The future for cigars . . .

Cigars might have faced a cloudy future but for the famous *Smoking and Health* report of 1964 and the subsequent studies linking cigarettes to several major respiratory and cardio-vascular diseases. The cigarette industry has tried to cast significant doubt on the findings but has failed to date. The report is itself cited as cause of the subsequent drop in cigarette sales.

No form of tobacco receives perfect marks in this milestone public health study. All tobaccos are associated to some degree with some physical distress. Cigars do receive high marks, however—praise by faint damnation in a sense. They can be linked only fractionally to some diseases, not at all to others.

Some excerpts dealing with cigars are comforting:

On total death rates (page 30) the 1964 report states: "Men smoking less than five cigars per day have death rates about the same as nonsmokers." The same paragraph *does* warn: "For men smoking more than five cigars daily, death rates are slightly higher."

Concerning the effects of smoking (page 31): "The risk of developing cancer of the lung for the combined group of pipe smokers, cigar smokers, and pipe and cigar smokers is greater than for nonsmokers, but much less than for cigarette smokers."

101

A 1967 follow-up study authorized by Dr. Luther Terry's successor, Dr. William Stewart, supported the 1964 findings. *The Health Consequences of Smoking* states on page 138: "There is relatively little risk of lung cancer associated with pipe or cigar smoking, probably because smoke from these sources is rarely inhaled."

These two reports must still be heeded. They represent the highest, most objective authority, and are the sources to which everyone interested in the smoking-and-health controversy must eventually turn.

New developments

What new developments can be expected tomorrow?

Most of the important strides will take place in growing and manufacturing technology.

■ New sources of all type of leaf must be found. "Filler is becoming the main problem," the aforementioned manufac-

turer states. There is simply not enough high-grade raw material
to meet the growing need.

■ New machines will appear and the need for the human
element in cigar making will shrink still further. An industry
spokesman says, "Total automation by 1975 is a possibility."

■ The small cigar rocket will continue to go up. Sales are
expected to top the one-billion-per-year mark and go right on
climbing. Standard classic types will probably fall in popularity,
however, and some big cigars may be phased out of production
altogether. A great deal of production potential is going into
small cigars. Even though panatelas are gaining in popularity,
for example, they are expected to rank considerably behind
the small cigars.

Will the three classic full-sized coronas, panatelas and
perfectos weather the changes blowing across the cigar industry?
Or will they eventually be cut back in production and lost in
the smoke clouds from mini-cigars?

Not likely.

102

The answer given by one of the world's busiest cigar
smokers to a different question several years ago applies here.

Curtis LeMay (World War II bomber command general,
Strategic Air Command chief, Vice Presidential candidate in
1968) has seldom been without a cigar in his adult life. He was
not without one the day he personally took up one of the B-36
bombers under his command.

The cigar troubled one crewman. He glanced at the glowing tip, fidgeted, then finally suggested that the general put it
out. What if a fuel leak developed? There might be fumes. The
general's cigar . . .

"The aircraft might blow up, sir," he said.

LeMay snorted, then said, grinning, "It wouldn't dare."

Those who make and market cigars would not dare predict
any critical blowup in custom-quality cigars. Such cigars, they
feel, will always be part of the good life.

"I would do anything to prevent their passing. If I didn't,
I wouldn't survive the beating my best customers would hand
me when they stormed the shop," one dealer said recently,
laughing. "Besides, if such a thing happened, there would be
nothing worthwhile left for *me* to smoke."

Tobacco Terms

AGING—the process of mellowing and enriching tobacco already cured. This is done by storing it loosely in hogsheads (see "breathe").

AIR CURE—to cure tobacco in barns under controlled ventilation without artificial heat. Fine cigar tobaccos are air-cured.

AROMA—the smell given off by fine tobacco smoke, especially important to cigar smokers. Pleasing aroma and flavor are the two basic qualities sought in cigars (see "flavor").

ASH—the residue of burned tobacco. Quality-cigar ash appears steely gray to white. Quantity of ash on a cigar is more important than color. Some ash (some experts insist that one inch is proper) should always tip a lit cigar. Reason: to disperse heat of the burning end.

BANKER'S CORONA—a type of English cigar manufactured in late 19th and early 20th centuries, noted for its intimidating large size and extraordinary cost. The price was about 12 shillings 6 pence each, or close to $3 at the value of the pound at that time.

BENT—the name given a square section of flooring in an air-curing shed.

BINDER—the layer of tobacco leaf rolled about cigar filler to hold or "bind" it together. In cigar construction the binder is the layer of tobacco between filler and wrapper (see "filler," "wrapper" and "homogenized tobacco leaf").

BLACK BEAUTY—any cigar wrapped in dark tobacco.

BLANKET—a cigar-manufacturing term for cigar wrapper leaf. Also, prison slang for cigarette paper.

BODY—the portion of a cigar between the head and tuck (see "head" and "tuck").

BOITE NATURE—any natural wooden box for storing cigars. The best are of Spanish cedar.

BREATHE—tobacco baled for aging and packed loosely so that air may circulate between the leaves so they can "breathe" (see "aging").

104

BROADLEAF—a descendant of native leaf grown in New England by Indians before English colonization.

BROOM—an old term still used for a low-priced cigar.

BROOM HANDLE—a slang term for a long cigar.

BROWNING—the second stage in air-curing cigar tobacco, following wilting, prior to drying. Leaves begin to turn brown at this stage due to evaporation of moisture (see "air cure," "wilting" and "drying").

BUCKEYE—any factory turning out products of varying and undependable quality.

BUG DUST—any cheap tobacco. Bug dust often turns up in cigars filled with scrap.

BULK—the name given any pile of tobacco leaves undergoing fermentation. A bulk contains from 3,000 to 5,000 pounds of leaf (see "fermentation" and "uniformity").

BULKING—the act of piling up filler leaves of different kinds to age together and achieve uniform taste and aroma (see "fermentation" and "uniformity").

BUNCH—the exact amount of filler needed to make one cigar.

BUNCO—any Philippine Islands cigar.

BUNDLE—a group of cigars usually without individual cello-phane wrappers, tied loosely with ribbons. Such cigars are round when smoked. They do not show the squareness exhibited by cigars pressed together in boxes. Bundled cigars are said to mellow with age as the result of loose packing. A bundle usually contains 25 cigars. A bundle is also known as the half-wheel. Many smokers consider two bundles in a cedar box the best form of cigar packing.

CABBAGE—any inexpensive cigar.

CANDELA—the designation for the light green tobacco used mostly for wrapper, now enjoying great popularity in the U.S. Leaf color and texture are controlled by heating dur-ing plantation curing. Candela is the Spanish word for "flame," an apt choice for tobacco cured by concentrated heat.

CEDAR—see *"boîte nature."*

CHAIR RUNG—the nickname given a large corona-shape cigar eight to nine inches long. This is also called a broom handle or double corona.

CHEROOT—a cigar now made of heavily fermented fire-cured Kentucky, Tennessee or Virginia tobacco. Long filler leaves are rolled in wrapper impregnated with rice-flour paste. The cheroot ends are trimmed and left open. The cheroot is slightly thicker than a pencil and is generally cut in half before smoking. The Tamils of southern India are said to have made the first cheroots. Their word for such a cigar is *shuruttu,* meaning "a roll."

CIGAR GIRLS—the women employed in the Spanish and Cuban cigar factories. Legend says that they rolled cigars on their bare thighs.

CIGARILLO—a small cigar, pencil-thin, four to five inches long, usually neatly made.

CLARO—a light-brown cigar leaf (see "coloring").

CLEAR—the word used for describing a cigar made entirely (filler, binder, wrapper) of West Indies tobacco.

COLORADO—a medium-brown cigar leaf (see "coloring").

COLORADO CLARO—a medium-light brown cigar leaf (see "coloring").

COLORING—the standard by which cigar tobacco (filler, binder, wrapper) is graded. There are seven basic colors. From lightest to darkest brown they are: 1. double claro; 2. claro; 3. colorado claro; 4. colorado; 5. maduro colorado; 6. maduro; 7. oscuro.

CONNECTICUT SHADE-GROWN LEAF—see "shade grown."

CONTINUOUS ROD PROCESS—a manufacturing method which produces a continuous rod of tobacco in cigar form, as rope is produced. The rod is cut into desired cigar lengths.

CORONA—a large-diameter cigar with straight, parallel sides, rounded head, cut tuck. Average corona length is about five and a half inches, but corona shapes are made in many lengths. Some are smaller, some larger than the above. The corona is one of the three basic classic cigar shapes (see "shape").

CROOK—a cigar pressed into a twisted, crooked shape. Sometimes called a "caduceus" because of its resemblance to the twisted snake staff of the Greek god Hermes.

CRUISE—when a cigar burns evenly following lighting it is said to cruise or to live.

CURE—to remove sap from tobacco leaf. There are several curing methods: fire cure; flue cure; air cure; sun cure. Type of cure employed depends upon type of tobacco desired. Pipe tobacco is cured differently from cigar tobacco, for example (see "fire cure," "flue cure," "air cure" and "sun cure").

CUSTOM—a term which denotes quality in cigars. The word is seldom used in its strict dictionary sense, that is, to denote a cigar made to a smoker's own specifications.

DEAD SOLDIER—a cigar or cigarette stub.

DOUBLE CLARO—One of the lightest (greenish-brown) of the tobacco leaves (see "coloring").

DRYING—the third and last stage after wilting and browning in the air curing of tobacco (see "wilting" and "browning").

END CUTTER—a sharp implement used to truncate or slit a cigar head to create free passage for smoke.

FERMENTATION—the important tobacco-processing step following curing. During this stage oils and flavorings are produced in tobacco leaf, as flavor and alcohol content are produced in wine during fermentation.

FILLER—the tobacco used inside the cigar. Filler makes up the cigar's greatest bulk (see "long filler" and "short filler").

FIRE CURE—to cure tobacco by drying it in smoke. This is one of the oldest curing methods (see "cure").

FLAG—the small flap of tobacco sometimes covering the head of a cigar.

FLAVOR—in cigar terms, the "taste" given off by natural sugars and oils in cigar leaf while being smoked. Artificial essences such as menthol are not considered true flavors. Pleasant flavor and aroma are the two basic qualities smokers seek in cigars (see "aroma").

FLUE CURE—a heating process which employs pipes, or flues, to radiate heat and dry tobacco (see "cure").

FOOT—the end of a cigar at which it is lit. Primarily known as tuck.

FORM—to arrange the exact amount of filler for one cigar in a "bunch" and mold or press it into the cigar shape desired (see "bunch").

FRONT MARK—the label on the front or end of a cigar box. This describes contents by manufacturer, shape, color, place of manufacture.

107

GLASS STORAGE—keeping cigars in airtight glass containers to ward off dampness in humid climates. This is a common practice in the Netherlands.

GRADING—there are two meanings to this word here: 1. for tobacco. Tobacco grading is simply determination of leaf quality, from lowest to highest. Grade level dictates use to which the leaf will be put. For example, thin, fine, elastic leaves receive high gradings. They are used primarily for wrapper. 2. for cigars. Selecting cigars according to color uniformity is known as grading. Good cigar graders take great pains packing boxes with cigars of one uniform color (see "coloring").

GUM TRAGACANTH—an adhesive used to seal the head, or mouth end, of a cigar.

HALF-WHEEL—see "bundle."

HAND—a bunch of tobacco leaves.

HEAD—the end of a cigar which is inserted in the mouth.

HOBO'S DELIGHT—a cigar butt, so called because of the notion that impoverished men spend much of their time exploring gutters for partly smoked cigars.

HOMOGENIZED TOBACCO LEAF—a tobacco product made of pulverized tobacco leaf, leaf ribs, sometimes stem parts (the entire plant except for the root). Binding materials are added to this pulverized material. It is then rolled into thin sheets resembling brown paper. Homogenized leaf is used for cigar binder and resembles brown paper. It is also called "sheet" or "reconstituted" tobacco.

HUMIDOR—a storage container, usually airtight and of wood, which keeps cigars fresh. The word is subject to loose interpretation. A tube holding but one cigar can technically qualify as a humidor. So can a storage room holding thousands of boxes.

IN CASE—a term indicating leaf condition. As long as a leaf remains soft and moist enough during curing to be handled, it is said to be "in case" or handling condition.

INDIANISCH WUNDTKRAUT—a common 16th-century European name for tobacco. The German expression means "Indian Wonder Plant."

KNOT—a bunching-up of filler at one spot in a cigar. A knot acts as a plug and impedes smoke passage.

LITTLE CIGAR—technically, a small cigar about the size of a cigarette with tobacco wrapper and shredded scrap filler. "Little" is used in this book to cover any number of the currently popular small cigars.

LONG FILLER—filler tobacco cut in lengths as long as the

cigar itself. Long filler is generally believed to be superior and is found in expensive cigars (see "filler," "short filler" and "scrap").

LONG NINE—a slim, long cigar. The number probably once referred to its length in inches.

LONG TOM—a long, slim panatela cigar.

LOOSE TWIST—a type of cigar made by loosely twisting tobacco leaves together and sold for two cents per handful to laborers building the railroads in the American West in the 19th century.

MADURO—a dark-brown cigar tobacco leaf (see "coloring").

MADURO COLORADO—a medium-to-dark brown cigar tobacco leaf (see "coloring").

MARRIAGE—the point at which different filler leaves aged together in a bulk have each borrowed enough of the other's flavor to produce filler tobacco of uniform taste (see "uniformity" and "bulking").

MATURING PROCESS—an aging step which follows manufacture of the cigar itself. This is an extension of the earlier tobacco fermentation.

109

NICOTIANA TABACUM—the scientific Latinized (from Jean Nicot) name for the tobacco plant.

NICOTINE—the alkaloid which gives tobacco much of its aroma and flavor. It is named after Jean Nicot who introduced tobacco to France.

NOODLE TWISTER—a cigar maker.

ODD LOT—a cigar so poorly made it is rejected for sale by the maker. Odd-lot cigars or "factory seconds" are rare items. Few cigars are manufactured so sloppily they can truly be called odd lots.

OSCURO—a blackish-brown cigar tobacco leaf, the darkest used in cigar manufacture (see "coloring").

PAPELITO—a small paper or husk tube filled with tobacco. Papelitos were once widely smoked in Latin America. They were contemporaries of early cigars and precursors of cigarettes. The word means "little paper" in Spanish.

PERFECTO—a medium-diameter cigar with cylindrical body, usually with tapered head and foot. The head is half pointed and closed. The tuck, or foot, can be either fully pointed or cut. The perfecto is one of three classic full-sized cigar shapes (see "shape")

PANATELA—a small-diameter cigar with cylindrical body. It has a rounded, open head and a cut tuck, or foot. This is one of three classic full-sized cigar shapes (see "shape")

PENNY PICKWICK—the term for inexpensive English cigars popular during the 1850s. They were presumably named after Charles Dickens' inquisitive and mobile Mr. Pickwick of *The Pickwick Papers.*

PIERCER—a spikelike instrument, often having an ornate handle, used for punching a small hole in a cigar head before smoking so the smoker will be able to draw.

POLE SWEAT—a form of deterioration which afflicts tobacco improperly ventilated while undergoing air cure (see "air cure").

110

PRIMED—in tobacco grower parlance, the leaves picked last from a plant are primed. Prime: another word for "pick."

READER—a person who literally reads to cigar makers while at work in their factories in order to alleviate boredom. Readers have all but vanished from American factories. They are still employed in Latin American plants.

ROBINSON CRUSOE—a discarded cigar butt, an outcast in the sense of Daniel Defoe's famous protagonist.

SCRAP—bits and pieces of tobacco leaf, sometimes stem. Scrap is used for filler in inexpensive cigars. Sometimes scrap is called "short" or "ribbon" filler (see "filler," "long filler" and "short filler").

SEGARRO—the Italian word for cigar.

SELECTOR—one who grades cigars according to color prior to boxing.

SHADE-GROWN—the tobacco growth process which takes place under acres of cloth tenting. This shading process is most commonly used in Connecticut Shade-Grown. This tobacco is light-colored, smooth-textured and used primarily for quality-cigar wrapper.

SHAPE—the basic contour of any given cigar. There are three basic or classic shapes today: corona, panatela and perfecto. Cigars are made in many sizes but usually are made in one of these shapes or some variation of one. In the corona shape, for example, there are petit coronas, half-coronas and so on, hundreds of expressions of individual manufacturer design (see "corona," "panatela" and "perfecto").

SHOESTRING—the name given a type of leaf grown in Connecticut early in the 17th century.

SHORT FILLER—filler tobacco of odd lengths varying in size and all shorter than the cigar itself. Short filler is considered inferior to long filler. It is generally put into cigars in the medium-to-low price bracket (see "filler," "long filler" and "scrap").

SHORT SIX—a short, homemade cigar. The number six probably refers to the length in inches.

SHOULDER—a tapering or drawing-in of a cigar at the head or mouth end. Any cigar so thinned is said to have a shoulder.

SNUFF—pulverized tobacco inhaled briskly through the nostrils, a pinch at a time.

SPILL—a wooden strip used for lifting tightly packed cigars from their box without damaging them.

STEM—removing the midrib from a tobacco leaf.

STICK—a piece of lath to which pairs of tobacco leaves are sewn. The stick with attached leaves is then hung from overhead bars in a curing shed. In Connecticut growers hang 20 to 22 pairs of leaves from each stick.

STOGIE—the cigar of the westbound pioneers, named after their sturdy wagons made in Conestoga, Pennsylvania.

SUCKER—the small shoot located low on a tobacco plant. Suckers tend to be poor-quality tobacco, are pruned often.

SUN CURE—to cure tobacco leaves by setting them in the heat of the sun to dry (see "cure").

SUN-GROWN—the term designating tobacco grown in the open without cheesecloth or other covering to provide artificial shade (see "shade-grown").

SWEATING—another term for the cigar tobacco fermentation process.

TABAQUERO—another Spanish word in the cigar lexicon. It means "cigar maker."

TORPEDO—a fat, almost football-shaped cigar with pointed and closed head and foot, or sometimes a cut foot. The torpedo is seldom manufactured today and almost extinct but once was a classic shape.

TUCK—the end of the cigar which you light. Tuck is occasionally called foot.

TURNING—the process of moving the outer leaves of a fermenting pile (bulk) to the inside, and the inner leaves to the outside, to induce even fermentation (see "fermentation").

TWOFER—the early 19th-century term for cigars selling two for a penny.

112 UNIFORMITY—the condition a blender of filler tobacco strives to achieve. He bulks (mixes) the various leaves in man-high piles. These leaves "marry," that is, ferment together, until they take on common aroma and taste throughout (see "marriage" and "bulking").

VEGA—the Spanish word for "tobacco plantation."

WEDGE CUTTER—a sharp implement which opens a wedge-shaped cut in the head of a cigar prior to smoking so that the smoker may draw.

WHIFF—in Europe, a small cigar, open at both ends.

WILTING—the first softening stage in the air cure of tobacco. The leaves literally wilt as moisture evaporates (see "air cure," "browning" and "drying").

WRAPPER—the outermost layer of the cigar, broad sheets of leaf wrapped about filler and binder to hold the entire cigar together.

ZIKAR—the Mayan word believed by scholars to be the root of the Spanish word *cigarro* and the English word cigar.